MW00817285

Goodbye Again

A MEMOIR
Adoption • Child Loss • Healing

CANDACE CAHILL

Joanne + Wayne
Thank you for your
support and love!
♡ Candace Cahill

Legacy Book Press, LLC
Camanche, Iowa

Copyright © 2022 Candace Cahill

Cover and author photos by Tina Graham
Cover design by Kaitlea Toohey (kaitleatoohey.com)
Lyrics have been included with permission from Roger Waters of Roger Waters
Music Overseas Limited and Administered by BMG Rights Management (UK)

In certain instances, names and identifying characteristics for entities and
individuals have been changed. As it is with all personal narratives, this one is
subjective. This story is told from the author's perspective and her memories;
she recognizes that everyone remembers events differently.

All rights reserved. No part of this book may be used or reproduced by any
means, graphic, electronic, or mechanical, including photocopying, recording,
taping or by any information storage retrieval system without the written
permission of the publisher except in the case of brief quotations embodied in
critical articles and reviews.

ISBN: 978-1-7375926-4-8
Library of Congress Case Number: 1-11414802971

For Michael.

CHAPTER I

Minnesota, August 1989
4½ Months Pregnant

The ragged edge of grimy linoleum between the kitchen and the living room snagged my sock. Again.

"*Shiiiiiit.*" I caught myself on the refrigerator handle while trying to disentangle the threads connecting my foot to the floor. "*Dam*mit!" They just continued unraveling. Once free, I yanked both socks off and threw them in the trash on top of a crumpled Doritos bag and a Coke can. Reaching over my newly emerged baby bump, I grabbed an old, deformed plastic glass from the cupboard and filled it from the tap.

"Okay, I'll go," I said to Eddie, my boyfriend.

He stood in the living room, frowning. "I just think we need to go into this with our eyes open." His greasy obsidian hair melded into a black Van Halen concert t-shirt, and his arms hung limply. He reminded me of a marionette.

The following day, I slumped onto an oversized loveseat at the counseling center. Eddie took the spot next to me and flipped open a copy of *Catholic Digest* he grabbed off the carved mahogany end table. The bitter aroma of freshly brewing coffee filled the waiting room, and above the single window, in three-dimensional lettering, a sign proclaimed: Caritas Family Services, Catholic Charities. Crushed red velvet upholstery stood out against honey-colored walls, and a bronze sculpture of Mary Magdalene stood sentinel in one corner. Suddenly self-conscious of my messy hair, tie-dyed t-shirt, and faded blue jeans, I crossed my arms and tried to disappear.

The putt-putt of the percolator ended abruptly with a final hiss just as a door opened behind the reception desk. A statuesque woman in a long, flowing blouse and loose, wide-bottomed trousers floated over to us.

"Candace, Eddie? Hi, I'm Joyce." In her mid-fifties, she exuded confidence and calm. Fleshy facial features and lips that curved naturally in a smile belied her brisk voice. "Very nice to meet you both. Please, would you follow me?"

I trailed Joyce and Eddie down a spacious hall with matching wood-framed mirrors that alternated side-to-side above waist-high wainscoting. I caught glimpses of myself every few feet. I'd let my permed auburn hair dry naturally, creating a straw-like halo that reached down to my shoulders.

Joyce waved us into her small office. Piles of paper and books littered every surface except the chairs, a contrast to the sparse luxury of the lobby. It felt…homey. Joyce took a seat behind the desk, a clipboard in front of her.

"I understand you're pregnant and trying to decide what to do."

Eddie nodded.

I shrugged, thinking about baby names. *I love the name Cameron. And Forest. Unique and artsy.*

"Well, I'd like to collect a little information, give you some educational materials, and make a plan for how our agency might be able to help. Interrupt and ask questions anytime you want, okay?"

I nodded, bringing my attention back to Joyce.

"How old are you two?"

"I'm twenty-one."

"Me too."

"Married?"

"No," we both rushed to answer.

"How far along are you?"

I twisted a strand of hair. "Almost five months. I'm due January 24th."

"Are you getting proper medical attention? Are you healthy?"

"The doctor says that other than low blood pressure and being underweight, I'm okay."

"Good. Can you each tell me, in your own words, how you think I can help?" She glanced at me first.

"He," I bobbed my head toward Eddie, "said we should come."

I didn't want to be there. I didn't need counseling to have a baby. Everybody has babies. But if Eddie wanted to explore how we could be better parents, I had to take him up on it. I'd seen too many friends and relatives abandoned by their boyfriends after getting pregnant, and I didn't want that to happen to me.

"Eddie?"

He leaned forward, one knee protruding from a hole in his Levi's. "Well, 'cause I don't know what to do. I never thought about having kids. I don't even know if I want kids." He shrugged. "And, well, I'm in college. I don't want to have to quit school."

"I know an unplanned pregnancy can be very scary," Joyce said. "I can help you consider your options. We can explore the details of parenting, including daily life and structure, how to budget, how you might deal with the stress of a crying baby–all of that. And we can look at adoption too."

"I don't want to give away my baby," I said, reeling back. "I don't thi-"

"I think adoption is probably the best way to go," Eddie said.

I gaped at him. *What the hell?*

Eddie and I had only known each other for seven months. We'd met while living in a co-ed rooming house near the university campus: half of the residents were college dropouts, and the other half were still trying to fit in classes between mushroom trips, beer bongs, and one-hitters. It was a late 80s version of a 60s flophouse.

Eddie seemed sweet and smart. A sci-fi and horror buff, he boasted a stellar collection of novels lined up next to a giant tank of piranhas in his dimly lit room. We'd lounged below his lofted bed, read comic books by the aquarium light, and smoked Marlboros.

Our relationship progressed quickly from friends to lovers and then moving in together. Eddie entered an in-patient drug rehabilitation program less than a month later at his parents' insistence, leaving me alone in our recently acquired, cheap, one-bedroom apartment. Two weeks after he left, breast tenderness followed by a visit to Planned Parenthood confirmed I was pregnant, and since my relationship with Eddie was consensual, I never considered abortion. When I told Eddie about the pregnancy during a visit to see him in treatment, his first question was whether I'd been on birth control.

I quit drinking and using drugs as soon as I found out I was pregnant, I told Joyce. "And then went to chemical dependency treatment, too—a different program than Eddie's. My social worker said it would be a good place to get prenatal care. I figured I could screw up my life, but it's not fair for me to do it to my baby."

Joyce nodded at me to continue.

"We wrote to each other almost every other day." I smiled, remembering Eddie's handwritten soliloquies. The thick envelopes, adorned with hand-drawn hearts and arrows, made my heart flutter, and trails of white confetti from the fuzzy edges of the spiral-bound sheets followed me wherever I went.

Joyce's voice jarred me from my reverie. "What are you doing to stay clean?"

"Going to NA, Narcotics Anonymous, a few times a week after class," Eddie said.

"Me too. After work, though." I'd gotten a minimum wage job at a local camera shop.

I didn't think either of us was an addict, but I was glad Eddie was sober. He had been especially helpful to me after we got out of treatment, making dinner and cleaning the cat box, but lately, his attention had been waning.

Maybe I was doing something wrong.

At the end of our scheduled hour, Joyce handed us each a "decision-making packet," encouraged us to do the first homework exercise and come back in a week or so.

Back at our building, I ignored the broken security door and took the stairs two at a time. The smell of mildew assailed me when I entered the apartment, and our meager furnishings made the spacious living room appear cavernous. Neither one of us had much to bring to the relationship.

"Do you want to work on this tonight?" I asked, waving the packet at him.

"Can't. I've got class." He stuffed a textbook into his backpack and slung it over his arm. He was studying architecture at St. Cloud State University. "Maybe tomorrow."

"Sure," I whispered to the door as it snicked closed. Eddie'd been spending more time on the university grounds or at his parent's house instead of coming home.

My mom and siblings lived over half an hour away by bus. I rarely saw them. I didn't know my dad. Well, I knew *who* he was but didn't *know* him. I'd met him only a couple of times after I turned thirteen.

The following evening, Eddie and I lounged on the tobacco-scented, second-hand sofa with Star Trek reruns playing in the background, each working on our worksheets. We positioned our bodies to protect our work like school kids. We didn't talk.

Two weeks later, back in Joyce's office, I squirmed at the tightness of my jeans and inconspicuously undid the button fly.

"Your goals are a lot alike," Joyce flipped through our worksheets. "You both want to attend college and work towards a career. And someday get married, but not right now. Eddie, you state you're not interested in being a parent yet, while Candace, you say yes, you want to be a mom."

"I don't think either of us is ready to be a parent," Eddie said, balancing on the edge of his chair. "Or even capable of it." His raven hair was just long enough to block his eyes from view.

What the hell is he thinking?

Joyce put down the worksheets, sighed, then turned to me. "As the mother, you have the first right to parent, and Eddie, you don't have much input. That's just how things are. It will come down to your decision, Candace."

I looked at the floor, then startled at Eddie's next words.

"That's not fair," he huffed. He slid back in his chair and crossed his arms. Under his breath, he mumbled, "My mom says I shouldn't be forced into this."

Forced? What's going on here?

At the end of the meeting, Joyce recommended individual counseling in addition to couple's sessions.

"I wanted to see you alone," Joyce said the next week, "because I sensed some animosity between you and Eddie." She tilted her head. "Did I read that right?"

"He's been acting kind of weird lately. We don't talk anymore." I glanced at my feet. "Not that we ever did, really. Things just feel…off."

I was doing something wrong; I was sure of it.

"Is he hurting you?"

"No. He just seems unhappy all the time."

"Well, this is a stressful situation. But let's shift our discussion and focus on you, shall we? Did you work on the next section of the workbook?"

"Yeah." I reached down, pulled it from my backpack, and handed it to her.

"What did you think of the budget exercise?"

I sagged back in the chair with a groan and ran a hand through my hair. "I had no idea how expensive babies were—diapers, formula, clothing. I've never even thought about how much it costs just for Eddie and me! We already go from paycheck to paycheck. How will we ever be able to afford it?"

"There are government programs that can help."

"No, I don't wanna live on welfare," I bolted upright, spine erect.

"There's nothing wrong with getting a little help," Joyce leaned toward me. "You're using medical assistance now, right?"

"Yeah, but that's different." Medical assistance was not like other types of welfare. *Welfare mothers milk the system,* Gene and his brother's derisive, mocking tones reached out from my childhood, and I didn't want to be one of *them.*

"Well, having put together a budget, covering food, baby supplies, rent, utilities, transportation, laundry, etc., you get a sense of the financial side of things. How do you feel about it?"

"There's no way we can do it, at least not with how things are right now," I rubbed the tops of my knees. This exercise had thrown me for a loop. "I'm thinking that maybe we could move in with my mom. She'd let us, I think. We wouldn't have rent or utilities and could pay for diapers and formula then. We'd have access to a washer and dryer, food, and she'd probably even babysit."

"Is it fair for you to assume she'll take care of you and your baby? And Eddie? That she'll pay for everything?"

I gaped at Joyce for a moment, then slumped back in the chair again. "No, I guess not." I never even considered how Mom would think or feel about it. "She's my mom; she's supposed to take care of me, right?" My heart dropped to the floor. "Crap."

"All right, hold on. I know it feels like the end of the world, but it's not. You and Eddie could move into a less expensive apartment. Sell your car and rely on public transportation. Apply for food stamps. There're lots of things you can do to make it work."

Easy for you to say. I slid down until my head came even with the chairback, accentuating my bulging tummy.

I couldn't stop from replaying a childhood memory:

Mom giving each of us kids two dollars in food stamps to buy something that cost just over one dollar so we could get quarters to do laundry. Then, spending hour after hour waiting in the sticky heat and oppressive din of the laundromat, avoiding the trash piled in corners and the stinky men sleeping in plastic chairs.

I didn't want to go on food stamps. Or welfare.

At our next meeting, Joyce suggested that knowing one's past could help shape the future, so I jumped right in.

"No, I don't remember getting the 'sex talk' from Mom. Anything like that was taboo."

Joyce had pulled her chair out from behind the desk to sit in front of me, open workbook resting on her lap. "How would you describe your relationship with your mom?"

"I don't know; she's my mom," I shrugged. "She doesn't work anymore since she married Martin. I'm glad because she's had it pretty rough." But I was stumped. I didn't know what Joyce wanted.

"She knows you're pregnant, right?"

"Yeah."

"What did she say?"

"Nothing," I shrugged again.

"Nothing?" Joyce seemed surprised.

"Yeah. What's she gonna say? My sister, Stacy, had my niece when she was eighteen. My cousin had her kid when she was seventeen. They weren't married. No big deal. It happens."

Joyce wrote something down on her notepad and then flipped back to the workbook. "You state here that you were sexually abused as a child. Can you tell me more about that?"

I sighed. I hated talking about the abuse. But Joyce was the counselor, and I was a good girl, so I took a deep breath and answered.

"My earliest memories are of being abused by my mom's second husband, Gene. It ended when I was twelve," I said, my voice monotonic. "My older sister, Stacy, spilled the beans when she entered rehab after she'd slit her wrist. The authorities sent me to a foster home and arrested him, but he was released right away. Got off scot-free."

Joyce set aside the booklet and leaned toward me; the scent of sandalwood emanated from her. "I'm sorry that happened to you."

Cracks appeared in my façade. A stabbing began behind my ears, and my heart hammered. I straightened in the chair.

"Did you get counseling?"

"Yeah." I swallowed and labored to block all feelings. "They forced us all to go to family counseling—together—it was such bullshit," I snapped. I could feel the flush that had risen to my cheeks, and I clenched my sweaty fists. "I don't want to talk about it." My stomach roiled like a rat was rummaging around inside.

"We don't have to. But I want you to know I'm here to listen anytime you want to talk. About anything, okay?"

"Yeah, okay," I whispered.

During the chemical dependency treatment program I attended months earlier, the therapists pushed me to address the sexual abuse, but I couldn't talk about it. Although it had ended years before, the wound festered, and the shame triggered automatic flight, fight, freeze, or fawn responses, just like the abuse did. Every time they brought it up, I shut down; it was there I learned the term "dissociate," and discovered I'd already mastered the technique.

"Let's take a closer look at some of this other family information, all right?"

I nodded and swiped away the escaped tears.

Joyce casually placed a box of tissues at the edge of her desk and then turned to a page in the workbook. It contained a series of boxes, and at the top of each box was a different title, including alcohol/drug addiction, abuse, violence, and neglect. Under each label were examples of actions and behaviors, and inside these boxes, I'd listed family members who exhibited those behaviors.

Joyce gently pressed me for more details, but I remained detached. Looking at the litany of names, upside down on her lap, appalled and embarrassed me. I folded in on myself, both physically and psychologically, wrapping my arms around my torso, and nestled my awareness into that quiet, white-blank space in my mind.

I left the session nauseous and light-headed. I stopped at the receptionist's desk and made an appointment for the following week but didn't keep it. I couldn't face the humiliation of my past and that Joyce now knew my deepest secrets - I wanted her to like me.

I alternated between dissociating from my feelings and ruminating in the days to follow on past horrors. I avoided Eddie and went to work where my co-workers seemed equally interested in minding their own business.

In late October, Eddie and I went over to his parent's house for dinner. I'd only met them once and thought they were intimidating – they were both professionals of some kind. Hoping to appear mature and dignified, I showered, blow-dried, curled my hair, and selected the nicest shirt that still fit. I frowned at my reflection, hating my freckles and ruddy complexion, and applied make-up to hide the flaws I saw everywhere.

Their three-story home was located near the lake, next to the university. Bold brick, clinging vines, and columns framed the porch. As I approached, the darkness near the doorway appeared unwelcoming and foreboding.

Tension sat at the dining room table like an unwelcome guest. Matching silverware clinked on plates and punctuated the silent meal, illuminated by three scentless candles nestled in the centerpiece. Afterward, we walked through a set of French doors to the sitting room, where a piano sat shrouded in darkness, bordered by dark wood bookshelves and recessed lights.

I gaped at the wealth.

"Candace," Mr. Beeker said, "we think you and Eddie should place this baby for adoption."

Jolted from examining the room's richness, I looked for Eddie, barely visible behind his mom.

"You and Eddie are not a good match," Mrs. Beeker spat, all pretenses at decorum abandoned. "And certainly shouldn't be starting a family or getting married."

"Who said anything about marriage?" I took a small step back.

She moved forward, her heels clicking on the hardwood floor. *Who wears heels at home?* "You both are too young." A perfectly manicured fingernail pointed at my chest. "There's no reason to throw your lives away."

"I'm not throwing my life away. What are you talking about?" I looked again for Eddie. "Eddie?" He remained silent as his parents both took another step forward. The floor-to-ceiling bookshelves loomed behind me.

"You just don't have what it takes to take care of a child. It's a lot of responsibility," she added. "You don't have a good job, no money, no support…" She let her words trail.

Backed into the corner, tears slid down my cheeks.

"You young people should be thinking about college and starting a career, not daycare and diapers." Mr. Beeker's tone contrasted hers, and he came off like a used car salesman. "We just want you to think about your future. And Eddie's future," he coaxed. "You don't want to keep him tied down, do you?"

I tried to get Eddie's attention, but his head was down.

"Just promise you'll think about it, okay?" Mr. Beeker said.

I nodded. What else could I do?

Me and Eddie silently walked back to the apartment. He led the way with drooping shoulders, his arms swinging loosely. Inside, my internal dialogue raged. I fluctuated between anger at being set up and humiliation, and by the time we got back to the apartment, the shame had taken control. *Yeah, I'm no good. Everyone can see it. No amount of make-up or nice clothes can hide the fact that I'm a piece of shit.*

Back in our apartment, I sank onto the couch, exhausted.

"I think we should place the baby for adoption," Eddie said, standing in the middle of the room. "I know you don't want to, but I do. I don't want to be a parent. I want to finish school and go on with my life."

A pressure in my chest turned to a thickness in my throat. "I'll do it on my own, then," my words came fast and hot. "My sister did it; I can do it too."

In early November, my belly preventing me from buttoning my jacket, I plopped down in Joyce's office. It had been over two weeks since our last appointment.

"Eddie and I broke up. He wants nothing to do with me or the baby."

No hint of surprise on her face or in her voice, Joyce asked, "Do you want to tell me what happened?"

"Well, Eddie's parents invited us for dinner last weekend. Afterward, they cornered me and told me I should place the baby for adoption. And Eddie just stood there!" My voice rose, and my hands balled into fists. "He hid behind his mom like he was in on it from the beginning! It's so easy for him just to walk away! It's not fair! What am I supposed to do? *I* can't just walk away."

Joyce leaned forward, put her elbows on her knees, halving the distance between us, and said, "You're gonna be okay."

I snorted. "I moved back in with my mom," but I didn't know what I was going to do now.

"That's a lot. Are you okay?"

"Yeah, I'm fine." But my constantly upset stomach and knocking heart said otherwise, and I'd not known where else to go. "I want to keep going. With the counseling." Joyce had always looked me in the eyes and listened to what I had to say. I'd come to appreciate her calming voice and easy nature, so different from anything I'd ever experienced. She hadn't shied away from me after I'd told her about the abuse, and she didn't make me feel small or insignificant. So, maybe, she *could* help me.

"You sure you don't want to talk about Eddie?"

"Nope," ending with a long hold on the "p."

"All right." She readjusted quickly. "I thought we could talk about how you feel when you're around children and how you interact with them."

"Well, I took care of my younger brother and sister a lot growing up, and now I babysit for my niece once in a while. A couple of summers ago, I took care of her for a whole week while my sister was out of town."

"How did that go? Did you have fun playing with her, reading to her?"

"Well, I thought it'd be cool, staying in Stacy's apartment, not having Mom breathing down my neck, but it turned out to be kinda lonely. We played games, yeah, and I read her books. We watched a lot of TV. Pretty boring, actually, when I think about it now."

"How did you handle it when your niece cried? Try to think back to how you felt?"

One specific memory unfolded in my mind:

Two-year-old Tara riding her tricycle through the sparsely fur-nished apartment, screaming merrily at the top of her lungs. Suddenly, a horrible smell fills the room. I look at her, spinning through the kitchen into the living room, and see diarrhea squishing out from both sides of her diaper! It fills the trike's plastic seat and runs down her legs. I watch as it flows to the wheels in slow motion and begins leaving tracks on the beige carpet. I scream at her, yell at her to stop, say she's a bad, bad girl. She starts bawling. I stomp over, grab her by the upper arm and drag her to the bathroom, still screaming, now in fear and confusion, and drop her into the bathtub.

"I felt trapped," I said, ashamed and unwilling to vocalize the memory. "I felt alone and scared. And bad. I felt bad."

During the rest of November, Joyce walked me through the remaining worksheets and topics on parenthood. We met weekly, and Joyce continued to encourage me to look at the reality of my situation. Every new topic heightened my anxiety and sparked visions of the future:

Me, alone in an apartment with my infant child. Trapped and fearful of how I'd be able to pay the rent, let alone buy groceries. Dependent on welfare, which, according to the voices in my head, made me a leech and a loser and a good-for-nothing whore, listening to the wail of a baby that hadn't let me sleep all night. Would I snap and cover my baby's head with a pillow to stifle the cries?

Living with my mother because I can't afford my own place, trapped in a basement bedroom with no window, a mattress on the floor, and a crib in the corner. A wailing toddler, with snot running down his face, screaming to be let out. Would I threaten to give him something to cry about?

Years down the road, feeling alone and desperate for companion-ship, would I unknowingly bring home a man I would later discover had sexually abused my child?

I roused from these visions, unable to breathe, sweaty, heart beating staccato. These were the patterns I'd seen my whole life. And all the worksheets I'd filled out, the materials I'd read, and the sessions with Joyce suggested it wasn't just possible but likely that I would repeat them. I felt doomed to fail. The counseling, which led me to dissect my family history, hadn't pointed out that I could *learn* behavior management or general life skills. And despite what I believe

were Joyce's best intentions for my baby and me, it had merely con-
tributed to diminishing my self-esteem. Naiveté prevented me from
understanding I could sue Eddie for child support, and he would be
obligated to comply. I didn't know what I didn't know.

"Okay, Joyce," I said, in early December, taking a deep breath and
leaning back, defeated, "I'm ready to learn about adoption. I know I
was scared to consider it, but, God… I don't know if I can be a parent!
And it's not just because I'm alone now," my throat tightened. Tears
ran down my cheeks, "I don't think I *should*."

CHAPTER 2

Early December 1989
7½ Months Pregnant

The following weekend, Eddie's mom called. She must have gotten Mom's phone number from Eddie, who I hadn't spoken to since I moved out of the apartment.

When I heard her voice, I quashed the impulse to hang up and took the handset into the bathroom, trailing the long, curly cord, and then closing the door for privacy.

"What do you want?" I pictured her smug face, eyes glaring over her red reading glasses like a librarian.

"Although I understand that this situation has been very difficult for you," her words belied the frost in her tone, "and as much as we do not want to add to your distress…"

Yeah, right.

"…we need you to know that if you keep this baby, we will fight you for custody."

I gasped. "What?"

"We do not believe you are in any position to take care of a child." Contempt saturated every word. "You're single; you're broke; you're alone. And, you don't have any support."

"My mom will help me, even if you won't."

"Well, we don't think your mom's a good role model." Her voice rose and fell derisively. "The years of abuse you've endured Candy, the alcoholism, the cruelty, the neglect… she will not help you be a good mother. She's not capable."

I was thunderstruck.

"Candy, listen. Your whole family is dysfunctional. And lacking — in everything. What do you think you can even give this child?"

Still and silent, I held the receiver glued to my ear as tears streamed down my face. Every accusation landed full force, like a boxer pummeling a punching bag.

"You know, Candy, any judge looking at you and looking at us will grant us custody. Eddie wants to place the baby for adoption. He will sign over his parental rights when the time comes. You should do the same." She hung up.

Nauseous and shaky, I staggered from the bathroom. Eddie's mom wouldn't place the baby for adoption if she got custody. No. She would keep the baby and purposefully lock me out, just to be cruel. My throat spasmed as I gasped for air. She would maliciously prevent me from having any say or access to my child. And if what she said about me, about my family, was true, what recourse did I have? I had no way to fight back.

I retreated to my bedroom, and sitting cross-legged in the middle of the mattress, spread the worksheets from my sessions with Joyce around me. *Am I that bad? Is my family? My mom?* As awful as Eddie's mom made me feel, her comments forced open a window I'd never been willing to look through: my own mother's role in the abuse. There, scattered in front of me, covering the pages of documents, was the evidence. It painted a stark picture. Although Mom was never physically abusive herself, she'd been negligent, and I could no longer ignore that Mrs. Beeker had a point. And like a tidal wave, Mom's failures washed over me.

When my stepfather sat me on his lap and fondled me under the table, how did she not see? What about when he bestowed on me inappropriate gifts, like negligée and fancy jewelry, when I was six, seven, eight years old? How could she have ignored those signs? When he crept into my bedroom, night after night, did she really sleep through it all as I'd always told myself she did? And, if she truly didn't see what was happening, what did that say about her as a mother? If she *did* recognize the red flags and ignored them, what then? Bile rose in my throat as pressure built between my temples.

Was she a good choice to help raise my child? She didn't protect me, so why would I think she'd do any better now? And, as if guilty by association, why did I think I'd be any better?

Motherhood will not turn me into something I'm not. I'll never be Suzie Homemaker or Mother Teresa, willing to sacrifice myself while baking a pie and keeping a clean house.

Nope. I'm more likely to slap my kid. Be angry I can't go to college or afford new clothes or a car. And I'll blame the baby.

I know I will.

I'll be frustrated by late-night crying and early morning feedings. Resentment and bitterness will build and build.

A powder keg ready to explode.

All that anger and frustration will twist and distort me, consume me, spread like cancer. Everything I touch will become toxic, my child most of all. That tiny human being will be a manifestation of depravity, sadness, and neglect. And all the while, I'll pretend things are all right. The people around me will sometimes wonder, but I'll weave a tale to make them believe. Because once it all begins, the shame I'll feel will prevent me from asking for help, and the vicious cycle will commence.

In the end, something horrible will happen.

I'll be the mother who drowns her own child in the bathtub.

I'll drive myself off a cliff or into a lake, with the baby strapped in the car seat.

Or, maybe, I'll just lock my child in a cupboard every day, twisting their perception into believing it's for their own good.

With each imagined transgression, I gasped, my body swaying as if struck. And although none of these things had come to pass, my mind made the leap, bestowing on me a title I didn't want: *Monster.*

In the end, as my legs dangled listlessly from the edge of the bed. I wept uncontrollably. I *wouldn't* be a good mother, and rather than destroy my child, I should do the right thing.

I must consider adoption. I had to, for my baby.

My despair and self-loathing escaped through lips drawn back in a grimace. To believe I was incapable of being a good mother felt like an ax cleaving my heart in two. I fought to stuff the emotions back inside because, deep down, I knew that I wouldn't be able to see a way forward if I didn't block the self-contempt eating my soul. I blasted Pink Floyd on my boombox, hoping to cover the sounds of my anguish, while spittle and tears filled the hands that cupped my face.

Then, as if on cue, the opening bars of "Comfortably Numb" burst through my misery. My head snapped up. I forcefully wiped the snot from my hands on the bedspread. And, as if I'd placed an ice pack against my hemorrhaging heart, the searing pain slowly gave way to stinging numbness.

"I'm still not sure I want to place my baby," I said to Joyce at our next appointment, voice flat and controlled, "but tell me more about adoption." I crossed my legs and watched slushy snow droplets plop from my boot onto the floor.

I did not mention the phone call from Eddie's mom, and since I had already put adoption on the table at our last meeting, it was easy to convince myself that what Eddie's mother said didn't matter. *I* was the one making the decision. And, latching onto this like a lifeline, I assured myself I was in control.

"All right. You know how we did the exercises to help understand the ins and outs of parenting? Now, we will do the same with adoption. Explore in-depth what that looks like, how it might feel, what the steps would be. And you'll have an opportunity to speak to other birth moms to get an inside perspective."

I maintained eye contact, but my body remained stiff. Although I was consciously choosing to move forward, I was still apprehensive.

"Adoption is a wonderful and beautiful alternative, but there are repercussions just like for parenting."

I listened, but half-heartedly. It was like a miniature version of myself sat atop my shoulder, voice incessant and unrelenting: *Adoption is what a good person, a smart person, would do.*

Joyce's long, beaded necklace swung forward as she leaned in. "Choosing to place your child with another family can be hard to do. You would feel sad. Very sad."

This is the high road. The logical choice, right?

"Are you listening to me?"

"Yeah," I said out of habit. Instead, my internal monologue continued to throw out phrases like punches.

If I keep my baby, I'll just cause pain.

"Mother's Day would be hard. And Christmas and your baby's birthday are commonly hard for birth parents too."

My baby deserves better…so much more than what I have to give…

"You can learn coping mechanisms. I can help with that, too." She paused.

I want my baby to be safe… and I want my baby to have a better life than what I had… It's not about me anymore; it's not…the selfless choice is to give my baby the best chance to succeed…

"No matter what you choose to do, Candace, to parent or place, you will spend the rest of your life reevaluating everything."

It's not about me…

We sat in silence for a time. I stared blankly.

"I haven't told you this yet, but I am an adoptive parent. My oldest daughter is adopted."

My head snapped up.

"And I can tell you from both personal and professional experience, adoption is complicated, but it is wonderful, too." Her face beamed. "There are so many couples who can offer a good life to your baby. Couples who can't have children of their own." Joyce clasped her hands together then spread her palms, "And now, with new laws in effect, you can even pick the parents; choose what things are most important to you."

I can pick the parents? I sat up straight. Such a seemingly minor detail created an immediate paradigm shift inside me.

Instead of wallowing in self-pity, I started thinking about what kind of parents I would want for my child. This was exactly what I needed to stop the negative feedback loop, and I latched onto it like a life preserver.

I left the session a different person. I strode confidently down the hall, eager to set up our next appointment. I had felt so powerless, but now a new sensation bloomed, one I never thought I'd experience in this condition: hope.

Before I even took a seat at our next meeting, I said, "I want to place my baby for adoption. It's already December. I'm eight months along. I don't want to delay the decision any longer."

Joyce smiled broadly. "All right, we can start by looking at what you want in adoptive parents." She pulled out a legal notepad. "But even though we may begin the selections process in earnest, you can change your mind up until the moment you sign away your parental rights."

"When will that be?"

"The soonest you can sign papers is twenty-one days after birth. That ensures you have had ample opportunity to reconsider and choose to parent instead." Her soft, motherly voice became crisp and serious as we talked about legalities.

I looked at my feet for a second, then blurted, "I want my baby to be placed with their new family as soon as legally possible. I want them to have a chance to bond right away." I would not waste a single precious moment of my baby's life. If I couldn't bond with him, I wanted his new family to.

Eddie and I met Joyce in a small, brightly lit meeting room at Caritas Family Services in late December. Joyce had suggested we choose the adoptive parents together. I resented his presence, but Eddie was still the father, and I figured he deserved a say.

"I have selected four couples for you to consider," she gestured to a pile of green folders on the conference table. "The couples represented in these files take into consideration each of your lists. And they are all willing to have open adoptions, as you requested, Candace, meaning they are prepared to meet you sometime after placement, just once, and provide updates each year until the child is eighteen years old."

Learning I could receive yearly updates had delivered the final incentive to choose adoption. I did not realize at the time how new this practice was, nor how contentious it could be for prospective adoptive parents. Most adoptive parents, I would discover, refused to maintain contact with first families, no matter how minimal or protected. Real and perceived fears, such as the first parents trying to take the children back or competition for the child's love, drove their desire to keep adoptions closed.

"Of course," Joyce added, "all correspondence must go through the agency to maintain the privacy of the parties."

The files contained headshots and a dossier of each couple. Also included was a letter from each potential parent generically addressed "Dear Birth Parents." The letters ranged in length from one to three pages, and all were typed, except one, which immediately caught my attention. The yellow legal pages contained messy penmanship scrawled in blue, marred in places by little globs of ink and crossed-out words.

> *Dear birth parents,*
> *I am writing you this letter so that you can better know me and my family. I am 35 years old, 6 feet tall, and 180 pounds.*

Thirty-five. Perfect.

> *I am also in excellent health. We live in a small rural community. I have worked in my present job for 15 years as a purchasing agent and traffic manager for our manufacturing facilities.*

Healthy. Mature. Established. Professional.

> *I enjoy being with people, and I'm very outgoing. I am a caring, sensitive, and optimistic type person.*

I glanced at Eddie and shook my head, my perspective soured by bitterness. *I wish he were like that.* He sat at the other end of the table with one folder in front of him, eyes scanning feverishly.

> *We practice the Catholic faith and attend our church regularly. My wife and I believe in bringing our children up in a strong Christian household.*
> *I attended college for almost three years and discontinued school because of the illness of my parents. I do strongly believe in seeing my children pursue whatever vocation they choose. They hopefully will choose to attend college or a technical school. Education is important to both of us.*
> *My wife and I have been married for 12 years. We have a 3-year-old son. My wife and I have always had an open and honest relationship. Our time together is special as we have always been each other's best friend.*

"Joyce, do you know if their other son was adopted?" I asked.

"Let me see." She checked which couple I was referring to. "Yes, right after he was born."

Having a sibling, or at least the desire for a second child if my baby would be their first, was high on my list. I leaned over the letter and tucked my hair behind my ears.

My wife and I grew up living close to each other in two very special families, so we knew one another long before we began dating. My wife is very understanding and easygoing, and we have always been very open about our feelings and needs. I think this is why we have always had such a great relationship and marriage.

We make our son feel good about his accomplishments and individuality. We both feel it necessary that our children feel confident in what they do and feel good about themselves as the person that they are.

We want our children to know the difference between right and wrong and to respect and treat all people as they would like to be treated.

We know we are very lucky, and we're grateful that we are able to experience parenthood. We are both generous people and have a hard time not spoiling our son a little. We look forward to our family growing as we feel it best to have 2 or 3 children so as they grow up, they can share their feelings about adoption and family memories.

I sat up straighter. *No secrets? How refreshing.*

We are a middle-class family and believe very deeply in the family unit. Our income is such that we can afford to have my wife at home raising our children, helping them grow in our family and as individuals so that one day they will have a healthy, loving family of their own.

I leaned back, the chair creaking, and lifted my eyes, dumbfounded. This guy seemed to have everything that I wanted. *Everything.*

My wife and I will be open with our children regarding their birth parents and help them become more aware of their heritage. We know that you also have many needs and questions concerning knowing what kind of people will be raising your child. I hope that this letter helps you become more aware of the type of people we are and that this will help make this very difficult decision easier. We both feel letters and pictures can be very rewarding and important for everyone involved. Any degree of openness will make it much easier for the one person that really matters, the child.

So goodbye for now.

All our love and prayers are with you.

Sincerely,

"Eddie," I extended the letter to him, "this is the one I want."

CHAPTER 3

December 1989
8 Months Pregnant

The late afternoon sunlight, low on the horizon as the winter solstice approached, streamed through the sliding glass patio doors at my mom's house. The warm rays caressed my bulging belly, and I set aside my journal to watch movement ripple across my abdomen. Fast-paced rhythmic bouncing, the baby's hiccupps, made me grin. For the first time since getting pregnant, I noticed what was happening in my body without being afraid.

After Eddie and I had agreed on the adoptive parents, I settled into a routine of working in the mornings, going to the library or bookstore on the way home, then reading, writing, and napping in the afternoons. Most evenings, I joined the family for dinner, slipping back into the familial rhythm from my younger years while I did my best to distance myself from Mom's volatile irritability.

My mom left Gene, her second husband and my abuser, three months after the sexual abuse surfaced the summer I turned thirteen. I did not acknowledge her reluctance to leave Gene because concealing my shame was priority number one. Relief that he wasn't my real dad and that I didn't have to face my schoolmates in the fall, who'd witnessed me pulled from class three days before summer break, overpowered everything else.

We'd sold most of our household possessions at the local flea market, and then packed what remained into the station wagon. The three-bedroom, basement apartment we moved into smelled of mold,

Pine-Sol, and urine. The transom windows offered little light, and concrete floors and brick walls sucked the room's warmth like a specter. But, to me, it was a vast improvement from the tiny trailer house of horror, where grasping hands and probing fingers filled my nights.

Taking care of five kids, aged two to fifteen, overwhelmed my mother. I became keenly sensitive to her anger and withdrew when she snapped and yelled. Later she would apologize yet justify her behavior because of how hard things were. She moaned endlessly under her breath about the lack of support and money from Gene, and I began to believe that if Gene hadn't abused me, we wouldn't have so many troubles.

I started to do everything I could in hopes of easing Mom's burden, and when my older sister, Stacy, moved out a year later, I slipped into a co-parenting role. Mom was diagnosed with epilepsy later that summer, so I obtained a waiver to get a driver's license, and at fourteen, became the family chauffeur. I took the younger kids to school, Mom to work, and did the grocery shopping.

Three years later, immediately upon graduation from high school, I moved out. I didn't even return to do laundry.

Since then, Mom had married Martin, a local university professor, and embraced being a stay-at-home mom. She now surveyed her domain from a captain's chair in the dining room of a split-level rambler while my younger siblings, Maggie, nine, and Bobby, ten, tore through the house like Tasmanian devils.

"Mom, Bobby won't quit bugging me!" Maggie screamed, running through the living room with her arms flailing, and then pounded down to the basement.

"You kids quit rough-housing." Mom said, her eyes never leaving her book.

Day after day, hour after hour, Mom sat at that table with a cup of hot water, an overflowing ashtray, and a messy stack of paperwork strewn before her like a puzzle. Her wispy ginger hair, tinged with grey at the hairline, resembled rusted steel wool. At forty-three, she appeared much older. Years of smoking had created permanent creases around her lips and turned her complexion grey.

"Whatcha doin'?" Bobby plunked down next to me on the couch, his chubby cheeks glowing from exertion. His breath smelled like sour milk.

"Writing."

"Whatcha writing?"

"A book. For my baby."

"Oh. Okay," he shrugged and slipped away, lumbering downstairs after Maggie, to watch cartoons on Nickelodeon.

None of my siblings spoke about my pregnancy or the impending birth, and neither did Mom or Martin. Not because it was off-limits, but because it was no big deal.

After I decided to place, I'd started the journal to give to the adopted family for my baby. I wanted to lay out my reasons for choosing adoption in my own words. I poured my heart into it. It was more a confessional than a chronicle as I shared my hopes and fears about the future. In hindsight, I was still trying to convince myself I was making the right choice.

Before Christmas, I ran into Tom, a friend I hadn't seen in over a year, at the mall. His chocolate-colored hair had grown long, curls stuck out in random places, giving him a wild, distracted look. He wore a trendy, color-block ski jacket and tight tapered jeans, accentuating his broad swimmer's shoulders and narrow waist.

"Oh my God!" he said as he bounded up to me outside Barnes & Noble. "You're pregnant!" Surprise played across his face and something else. Regret, I think. He smiled, showing off metal-free teeth. "You look amazing!" he said as his eyes reached mine.

We had worked together at a café when we were both seventeen. He'd been a senior in high school, and I was a newly emancipated college student living in a shared rental.

"Long time no see," I grinned.

He reached for a hug, awkward because of my tummy and the distance of time, but his embrace was warm, soft, and full.

We'd spent countless hours at my place after work listening to Pink Floyd and Grateful Dead albums, sharing a set of big headphones so as not to wake my roommate. Less often, we went to his place, where we played his dad's guitar and talked conspiratorially on the sofa. His parents didn't seem to like me, and I thought it was because of my fishnet stockings, black eyeliner, and potty mouth, but in reality, it was because Tom already had a girlfriend.

"How are you?" I asked; the scent of Paco Rabanne lingered in the air between us.

"I'm good! Just home from The Cities for the holidays," he motioned to his mom several yards away. "How are *you*? Other than pregnant, of course!" He chuckled.

Tom was a big flirt—flamboyant, confident, and demonstrative—but he'd also been a nerd who buttoned his shirts up to his chin and wore braces. Now, he appeared to have embraced a trendier persona. I smiled, remembering our late-night phone conversations about everything and nothing into the wee hours. He had a girlfriend away at college, and I tried to lure him from her, using sultry tones, but in the end, she knew I was a threat and gave Tom an ultimatum: her or me. He chose her. Although disappointed, I wasn't surprised—I never considered myself good girlfriend material.

"I'm all right. Not much new, I guess, other than this." I pointed to my stomach.

"Can I come see you? Tomorrow maybe?" he asked.

My eyebrows rose, "Yeah, sure."

The following morning, I vacuumed and tidied up, then watched the driveway over the top of my book. I kept reading the same page over and over.

When he arrived at the door, he followed me downstairs. The family room was a musty space, long and rectangular with dark paneling, forest green carpet, and thick, thermal drapes that hadn't been open in years. We sat on the sofa, facing the TV, VCR, and Nintendo game console crammed in the middle of a bookshelf strewn with toys, books, and knick-knacks.

I asked him the standard catching-up questions, and the conversation remained on the surface – until Tom blurted out, "What are you gonna do?"

"I'm going to place the baby for adoption." I held his gaze, confident in my choice but wary and uncertain how he'd react.

"Wow, really? That's," he paused, "amazing." He shifted his body to face me, angling his knee on the sofa between us, and placed one arm casually over the back of the couch. "Brave."

Tentatively, I gave him a recap: my relationship with Eddie, our falling out, the eventual move back to Mom's, and the decision to place my baby for adoption. I concealed my emotions for as long as I could but began to tear up at the end.

I expected him to recoil in shock and contempt. Instead, he reached for my hand, laced his fingers with mine, and waited while I regained my composure.

Several minutes later, he leaned toward me and moved both hands to cup, but not yet touch, my belly. "Can I feel?" He asked. The sympathy in his vivid blue-green eyes caught me off guard, and I lost it; tears resumed as if they'd never stopped.

I nodded.

No one had touched me in months. I began to sob.

After a while, he backed into the corner of the couch and swung one leg up, motioning for me to sit in front of him. Then he gently pulled my back to rest against his warm chest. His arms slipped under mine, and he rested his hands on my belly.

Cocooned in his embrace, we sat in silence.

When he finally got up to leave over an hour later, I knew I wouldn't see him again. He'd go home, enjoy Christmas with his family, and then head back to college. But he'd given me something precious, something I didn't even know I was yearning for: acceptance, unconditional love, and physical intimacy.

The holiday season passed in a haze. I worked, read books, and began attending a support group for young pregnant women planning to place.

I became friends with Lisa, who was two years older than me and due around the same time. She lived nearby, so I caught rides with her to the group. She was married but already had four children, so she and her husband planned to place the new baby for adoption. We laughed at our shared experiences of explosive gas and unbearable heartburn and cried for the future.

Just after the new year, at eight months along, Lisa's baby died in utero. I accompanied her to the hospital, where she delivered a stillborn girl, and then sat dry-eyed in the corner as she and her husband said goodbye to the baby. I tried to picture myself in her shoes but recoiled from the guilt I thought she must feel. If Lisa hadn't been planning to place her baby, maybe she would have lived. I obsessed about the same thing happening to me, certain I deserved it. But Joyce, using soft sing-song tones and calm words, helped me focus and reassured me that everything would be okay.

At 6:00 a.m. on January 19, 1990, my alarm went off as usual, but I realized something was different as soon as I opened my eyes. I shifted into a sitting position, and a tightness in my lower abdomen spread to my whole body. Relief and excitement coursed through me as I grabbed my robe.

When I came upstairs, I found Mom perched at the table. "My contractions have started."

"How far apart are they?" She asked, blowing smoke out of the side of her mouth. A fluffy, pink robe covered her fleece pajamas, and she wore wool socks inside her slippers.

"Not sure."

"You better start keeping track. Here," Mom tossed her to-do list from the day before at me, "use the back of this."

I kept track of the contractions while preparing to go to the hospital. I took a quick shower-contraction-curled my hair-contraction-applied mascara-contraction. I packed a paper bag with deodorant, a toothbrush, clean underwear, and a sweatsuit. Mom didn't appear concerned when I walked through the kitchen at random intervals, so neither did I.

When she deemed it time, we put our coats on and headed out the door. We didn't talk about her giving me a ride; we both assumed she'd go with me.

The harsh odor of disinfectant assaulted me when I entered the delivery room, all sharp angles in white and chrome. The only color was a light blue tissue box with a tiny silhouette of a blackbird on the side. Mom took control, brushing aside the nurses whenever she could get away with it. She rubbed my lower back between contractions, and then when one hit, she held the image of the tiny bird mere inches from my face and told me to breathe. I'd had no Lamaze classes or any other preparation, but Mom was there, and I reveled in the unexpected protection and closeness I felt.

Late into hard labor, after pushing unsuccessfully for an unknown amount of time, Mom's voice came out of the fog, sharp and angry. She demanded something, but I didn't know what, and would later learn she yelled at the doctor that I needed an emergency c-section. The next thing I knew, I was rolling into the elevator with Mom next to the gurney, stroking my hand.

"Millions of women do this every day, Cand; you'll be all right." Her voice drifted softly in a world tinged with scarlet as I floated into drug-induced oblivion.

I woke in a haze of paranoia; certain I was naked in a crowded room. Instead, I found myself in recovery. Mom stood above me and touched a lock of my hair that had slipped from the hairnet. "They let me hold him…he's perfect," she whispered, a tear dripping down her saggy cheek.

I faded back into unconsciousness.

When I woke again, I was alone in a patient room. Hazy artificial light from commercial outdoor bulbs filtered through the bottom edge of the closed blinds, letting me know it was nighttime. A nurse visited briefly, then the dim lights and hum of medical equipment lulled me to sleep.

In the morning, they brought my baby to me. Little pursed lips and rosy cheeks peeked out from the hospital-issued garb. Gently, I touched a circular bruise on the crown of his head, barely visible under the fuzzy strawberry-blond hair.

"That's just from him trying to come out," the nurse said, with an amused lilt in her voice. "Don't worry, he'll be fine; there won't be any lasting effects." She finished checking the IV and noted my vitals in the chart. "I'll leave you with him for a bit before I take him back to the nursery. Just ring if you need anything."

"Hello, baby boy," I whispered. "I'm sorry if I hurt you," I stroked the bruise on his head. "Are you okay?" I moved to caress his tiny hand, then nudged my finger into his little clenched fist, which he instinctually grasped. "I think I'm going to name you. I know your new family is just gonna change it, but I can't let you go nameless. What do you think?"

His rosy complexion, dusted with tiny newborn pimples and fuzzy halo of hair, reminded me of a cherub, and I smiled despite myself.

"Do you like Forrest or Foster?" I asked as if I expected him to respond. "And Cameron? I've always liked that name." I rattled on, throwing random names into the ether. In the end, I chose Foster Cameron.

I recuperated in the hospital for four days, the extended stay necessitated by the cesarean section. I was grateful the other bed was vacant—it was hospital policy to allow for single occupancy on the maternity ward, if possible, in an adoption situation. I held my son, rocking him gently, and marveled at his perfect little ears and tiny fingernails. I refused to waste what little time we had together and observed every detail. Once, with the door to the room securely closed,

I bared one breast and brushed my nipple across his cheek. He turned, instinctively, and latched on, hungry for life's milk, and I was eager to give it, but I forced myself to stop—my internal critic screamed that I should not breastfeed him if I wasn't going to keep him. I did not want to interfere with his ability to bond with his new family.

There were no flowers, cards, or balloons, which was all right with me—I didn't deserve any.

"Knock, knock," Joyce said as she strolled into my room. "How's your recovery coming along?"

"All right, I guess. We're being discharged tomorrow." I didn't look up from rocking my son.

She eased into the extra chair and peered at the little bundle in my arms.

"What are you thinking today?" she asked, her voice husky.

Joyce wanted to know if I'd changed my mind. She had told me that seeing my baby might shift my perspective, that it was not uncommon for a placement plan to disintegrate the moment the mother set eyes on her child.

"I've gone over everything; again." I paused as my throat threatened to close. "And I can't be a parent. I just can't," I choked.

I labored to breathe and tried in vain not to cry. Tears fell off the tip of my nose, and landed on his blue blanket, then vanished.

Our days together had been both beautiful and terrible. I'd held my baby, sung to him. I'd kissed his tiny fingers and toes and breathed in his intoxicating infant scent. I'd immersed myself in the connection between us; I felt it keenly and through my entire physical being. But I didn't change my mind. And just like I learned to do from a past full of neglect and abuse, I sectioned off feelings of attachment to my infant and closeted them away.

I did this to protect him and to protect myself.

CHAPTER 4

January 24, 1990
5 Days Old

Early Wednesday morning, five days after childbirth, I prepared to leave the hospital. I knew this would be the hardest thing to do so far, but I had a plan. I asked the facility social worker to come to my room.

"I need you to be sure that I'm gone before you give him to the foster parents," my words tumbled out as soon as she entered. "*I* need to be the one to walk away. I can't risk feeling like they took him from me. Do you understand?" I pleaded, leaning forward, hands clenched into fists, barely holding my tears in check. "Don't let them *take* him from me."

"Yes, I can do that," she nodded, her brow furrowed sympathetically. "I'll be there with you when you leave the hospital, and I'll take care of everything."

Later that morning, exit plan in place, I was ready to face my decision.

I wanted to relish the last opportunity to see him - soon, he would no longer be "mine" - and asked if I could prepare him for departure. Joyce agreed and brought me the infant car seat, diaper bag, and blankets the foster parents had provided.

Collecting my baby boy from the nurse, I laid him on the changing table. I ran my fingers over the soft, almost colorless fuzz on top of his head, then unwrapped the blue waffle blanket which cocooned his tiny body. He'd already lost most of the newborn wrinkles, and his cheeks were full and glowing. I kissed his smooth forehead and let my lips linger while the warmth emanated from him into me. Tears slid down my cheeks as his hands, freed from the blanket, waved in the air.

"You deserve so much more than I can give you," I choked. "This is for the best." The words came out as if I were trying to burn them into his soul.

34

His head turned toward my voice, and his arms ceased moving. Stillness settled over the room.

"I'm sorry I can't keep you. I'm sorry I can't be your mom. Oh, how I wish I could, but I can't."

His dark grey eyes seemed to stare knowingly into my soul. Then his tiny fingers, topped in razor-thin fingernails, closed into a fist, and it felt as if they wrapped around my heart.

I jerked myself upright, fighting to reject the nausea and crushing pressure in my chest. I rewrapped him securely in the new blanket then tucked him carefully into the car seat. Taking a steadying breath, I slipped his first blanket into my paper bag, and I gazed down at him one more time. I didn't beg for forgiveness, and I didn't promise him anything. I just said goodbye.

Swiping my eyes, I placed the car seat in the social worker's arms, then gingerly sat in the obligatory wheelchair.

The social worker kept pace, silent and stoic as we wheeled to the elevator. *I can do this.* I wiped away snot with my sleeve. *I am doing the right thing — for both of us.*

When we reached the lobby, the social worker stopped at the reception desk and placed the car seat atop while I rolled onto the entrance.

I didn't look back. I couldn't.

Lisa waited for me just outside the sliding doors, car idling. She came around to the passenger side. "Are you all right?" She reached her hand to help me stand: the stitches were nothing compared to the heaviness in my chest.

I nodded, resigned.

As I got out of the wheelchair, the foster parents pulled up behind us in the arrival/departure area. I had met them just two days prior, but I slid resolutely into the car, refusing to acknowledge them. The weight of my decision fell like a boulder in a pond and landed in the pit of my stomach, leaving ripples I thought would never dissipate.

The car's bald tires spun on the icy street as we exited the parking lot.

"How are *you* doing?" I finally asked, pulling myself out of my sorrow.

"Sad." Her profile stood out against the bright daylight that streamed through the car window. A trickle escaped out of the corner of her eye. "Yeah, just fucking sad."

She'd been incapable of coming to the hospital to visit me, her pain so raw, and I hadn't been sure she'd come to pick me up until she answered my call that morning. The intensity of our shared grief—mine fresh, hers less than a month old—bridged the space between us as we held each other's hand over the center console. There was an awful comfort in knowing I didn't have to explain. I wish I'd realized the significance of that moment, how that unspoken solidarity brought a level of support like nothing else would for years to come.

Once at Mom's, I carefully slid out of the car, legs first. Lisa offered me her forearm, and I hoisted myself up out of the vehicle. She hugged me gently, then left. What else was there to say?

An oppressive silence greeted me when I entered the house. I used the hand railing to descend to the basement, closed the bedroom door, and pulled out the baby blanket. Delicately, I lay down and rolled onto my side, mindful of the stitches, and bunched up the blanket under my cheek like a pillow, losing myself in the smells of baby powder and infant formula.

I refused to surrender entirely to the grief, though. There was still the mandatory twenty-one-day waiting period, time yet for me to change my mind before the adoption agency could place my son with his new family. So, while he was in foster care, I allowed myself to cry in the privacy of my room. But only occasionally. Instead, I tried to shut down my emotions. I told myself I should be happy he would be going to a "good family," but happiness was the furthest thing from my heart.

I kept busy finishing the items I planned to send with him into his new life. I'd drafted a 24" x 52" composition with the lyrics to "If I Had the World to Give" in Uncial calligraphy, surrounded by a floral border in pastel chalk. My protruding belly had prevented me from holding the calligraphy pen correctly, so I worked to complete the inking. I also made the last entries in the journal, taped a snapshot of myself inside the cover, and set aside my favorite ring as a keepsake.

One evening, about two weeks into the waiting period, I joined my family for dinner. The kids talked and laughed while Mom presented fried chicken, mashed potatoes, and green beans. Voices hushed once Mom joined the table, and Martin, a devout Catholic, said grace. After the dishes sailed around the table, we dug in.

Then, the telephone rang.

Bobby leaned back in his chair and grabbed the phone off the wall. "Hello? Yeah, just a sec," he said and handed it to me.

I got up and walked into the living room, "Hello?"

"Hi Candace, this is Janet, the foster mom. We think the baby is colicky, and we'd like your permission to take him to the doctor, just in case."

"Colicky? Of course, yes," I replied urgently, "Please, take him in right away."

"Thank you. We will. He's doing well otherwise. I just thought you'd like to know."

"Thank you." I didn't know how else to respond. I replaced the receiver on the wall base and sat back down, grateful the foster parents took their job seriously.

Suddenly, Mom bolted out of her chair, scraping it harshly across the floor. She was shaking.

As she stalked away from the table, she said over her shoulder, in a barely audible snarl, "He should be here, with us so that *I* can take care of him."

Her reaction came as a complete surprise. She'd made no comments, positive or negative, regarding my adoption plan. None. But clearly, she was not happy. I sat there with my mouth open, along with the rest of the family.

I didn't anticipate an explanation, but I was at a loss. What did she expect?

She said nothing else to me that night after the foster mother called or any other time during the rest of the waiting period, and I did not seek her counsel. I hunkered down in the basement, the door to my room—and my heart—closed.

On February 8, 1990, I took the Metrobus to Caritas Family Services.

The receptionist ushered me to the same conference room we'd used when choosing the parents. This time, Joyce sat next to an overweight man in a dull grey suit and bright red tie, a sheaf of paper held together with a giant paperclip in front of him.

"Are you doing okay, Candace?" she asked.

"Yeah," I answered automatically. I placed the journal, artwork, and small jewelry box on the extra chair then took a seat. "This is the stuff I want the adoptive family to have."

I crammed mittens in the pockets of my coat and slipped it off, then bunched it behind me. Now that I was here, I just wanted to get it over with.

"Okay, I'll be sure they get everything," Joyce said. "Eddie came in earlier and signed away his rights already."

I nodded. *I guess he got what he wanted.*

"This is Mr. Levey. He's the agency attorney. He has the relinquishment documents ready for you to sign."

He pulled the paperclip off and slipped the first of several pages in front of me.

"This one," he said, passing me a fat ballpoint pen, "gives up your parental rights."

Dry-eyed and numb, I bent over the table. Careful to use my best penmanship, I resolutely signed.

Mr. Levey collected the page, then handed me three more. "These concern your desire for contact once the baby is placed. The first one is for updates and states you want one at six months of age and then once a year until he's eighteen."

I read the contents with cold, focused attention, then signed.

"This one expresses your desire to meet them after the adoption is finalized. Joyce will make the arrangements when the time comes. And the last one gives your consent to keep your file open here at the adoption agency in the event the child decides to seek you out. If you ever want to close your file, you must contact the agency to file new paperwork."

"Did Eddie keep his open?" I asked.

"No. And he didn't request any updates."

Documents in hand, Mr. Levey tapped them on the tabletop, and once aligned, put the paperclip back on. As he stood, he said, "That will be all. Thank you for coming in today."

It took less than twenty minutes to give away my son. He would be with his new family by the end of the day.

After the attorney left, Joyce asked if I wanted to stay for a while, but I declined. I just wanted to go home. She walked me to the reception desk and said, "I'm here whenever you want to talk, okay?"

I nodded and pushed open the glass door. Tears sprang to the surface and scorched down my face as the door slid closed behind me. Snow crunched underfoot on the partially cleared sidewalk as I walked back to the bus stop, head hunched forward beneath my raised hood.

It's done.

On the bus ride home, I sat with my forehead pressed against the cold window, averting my face from strangers to hide the flood of emotion. I was glad the window was frosty – I didn't want to see my reflection.

While I walked the two blocks home, I wept openly; my sobs resonated over the winter bird songs. I opened the door, climbed the stairs, and stopped in the middle of the dining room. My arms hung limply as tears dripped off my chin.

Mom, who leaned like a tripod on the kitchen counter, didn't even look up. "He's dead to me now," she said, and then turned and walked away.

I stepped back as if struck. What little air I had, whooshed from my lungs. The tears and gasps stopped abruptly. I slunk down the stairs, packed the essentials, and left. I wasn't sure where I would go, but there was no way I was staying there.

I hadn't maintained many friendships while dating Eddie or since we broke up, but I called Helen, an old high school buddy from a payphone at the mall. She agreed to let me crash on her couch and even brought me food and Kleenex but otherwise left me alone, as I'd requested.

On the upper floor of a private residence, her apartment had a sturdy loft-ladder to the single bedroom. Thick wooden beams vaulted the ceiling like an exposed skeleton. The blocky wood couch created a casket-like trough for me to hide in, its cushions musty and lumpy. An old quilt and a bunch of mismatched throw pillows created a nest for the duration of my stay. Other than going to the bathroom, I rarely left the sanctuary of the sofa: eating, sleeping, crying.

Hours passed in blank-white, quiet stretches of numbness, followed by solemn bouts of crying when self-pity and loathing coursed unchecked down my cheeks.

I deserve to feel this. I'm a horrible mom. No, I'm no mom at all. I deserve this.

Over and over in an endless loop, and I surrendered willingly. I screamed too: pillows held to my face in attempts to stifle the sound while slimy tracks of saliva oozed from my gaping mouth and clung to the fabric in streams.

I railed at Mom. I needed her, but where was she? The pendulum of emotion swung between the sting of betrayal and the aching desire for someone to hold and comfort me. An instinctual yearning for "mommy," despite the evidence she wasn't up to the task, triggered a return to the self-loathing for the same reasons.

After a week of surrendering to my feelings, a lightness, like a bubble of air, seemed to surround me. My senses heightened, and I felt cleansed, open. I could smell the remnants of bacon from the day before and practically taste the crisped edges. The tick-tock of the clock felt as though it were inside my skull, ricocheting like a racquetball. The sky visible out the window wasn't just blue; it was shades of cornflower, cobalt, and indigo.

I called Joyce.

"I left Mom's, and I need some place to go."

"Are you safe? Where are you?"

"I'm crashing at a friend's, but I don't want to stay much longer."

"Okay, let me look around and see what I can find. I'll get back to you later today or tomorrow morning at the latest. Are you okay?"

"Yeah, I've been...processing, I guess. I'm sad, but I think I'm okay."

"Okay," she hesitated, but her tone indicated she had something to add. "I know you wanted to know, and I just received word from the adoptive couple on the name they've chosen: Michael Ryan."

Tears sprang to my eyes, and a sudden thickness in my throat threatened to suffocate me. I thought I'd be happy to learn his new identity, but instead, it was as if another piece of him had been taken away.

"A good Irish Catholic name," she added softly. "You should come to the birth mother's support group this week. I think it would be good for you."

I remained silent on the line.

"You don't have to say anything."

"All right. I'll go."

She called the next day saying she'd found a good possibility, but it would be a week before she'd know anything for sure. During that time, though, she suggested I go to a place called Clare's Well. It was a farmstead run by a couple of Franciscan nuns, a rural retreat center for reflection and recovery. Joyce arranged for me to go at no charge, and I had nothing to lose. And nowhere else to go.

After a forty-five-minute drive into the rural countryside, Joyce and I turned onto a long, winding driveway. A red barn, John Deere tractor, and several small outbuildings lined the yard's perimeter. A crisp white farmhouse sat atop a small hillock. The large kitchen, smelling of baked bread, greeted me beyond the arctic entry. The wood floors creaked underfoot.

A plump woman with wiry grey hair greeted us at the door, and after sending Joyce on her way, she led me through an arched hallway that doubled as a library to a private bedroom upstairs. A writing desk, lamp, and chair stood next to the window, and a thick, colorful quilt covered the twin bed.

Later that afternoon, snuggling on the couch in the living room under a crocheted afghan, I gazed out the picture window. Bent brown grasses and low shrubs encircled a frozen pond, and snow-covered fields spread out as far as the eye could see. The wood inside the potbellied stove hissed and crackled.

During the following week, I spent long days writing in a new journal and reading the magazines and books from the library. No religion or spiritual tradition was off-limits here, a surprising and welcome discovery. There were books on Buddhism and Paganism, a copy of the Quran and Torah. I even found a deck of Tarot cards on an end table: Daughters of the Moon. This place was not at all what I'd expected.

And neither were the nuns.

As a child, Catholic grade school had exposed me to the rigid control and harsh discipline of Augustinian nuns. I had my mouth washed out with soap or hand whacked with a ruler too many times to remember. But I didn't realize there were other sects. Here, the nuns wore regular clothing and talked like ordinary people - no *thee's* and *thou's*. I was shocked the second morning when Sister Agatha came downstairs in nothing but a towel; no, these were not the nuns of my childhood.

"Would you be interested in getting a full body massage?" Sister Agatha asked me on the third day. "I'm a certified massage therapist. It's one of the ways we make money out here - I have clients from all around the area."

I raised my brows.

Seeing my confused expression and misinterpreting it, she added,

"There wouldn't be any charge to you if you want to have one."

"I've never had a massage. What's it like?"

"Here. Come downstairs, let me show you."

The basement was musty, not unusual for Minnesota, but bright with light. Heat lamps lined the wall at the bottom of the stairway in a makeshift greenhouse. Beyond a plastic curtain, the basement opened into a spacious room with grey brick walls and concrete floors covered in throw rugs and carpet remnants. Multiple accordion-style privacy screens cordoned off a professional massage table along the wall farthest from the stairs.

"I just had a c-section, and my stitches are still healing. Can I still get one?"

"Sure, as long as it doesn't hurt to lie on your stomach."

During the massage, Sister Agatha noted areas of tension, easing my muscles with practiced pressure and strokes. She talked freely and softly, without shame or derision for my naked form, which I'd felt for myself since old enough to remember.

"You're really tense in your quads. Most people hold traumatic childhood memories here, so don't be surprised if you feel emotional. And if you feel like crying, go ahead; it's natural, it won't bother me." Her voice was like velvet, caressing me along with her skilled hands, and tears flowed. "You have every reason to cry, dear. And you *need* to cry. That's good. Go ahead, just let it all go."

So, with her permission, I did.

By the time I left Clare's Well, a week later, I was a changed woman. I felt a sense of safety and serenity I'd never experienced until I was under the watchful eyes of these women of faith. I was no longer a believer, having turned away from the religion I thought misogynistic and cruel. But I recognized the significance of their presence. They encouraged me to do whatever I needed to grieve and heal and did so without judgment or dependence on any one specific doctrine. At the Well, I didn't feel judged for my past or who I was as a result. These women stood as role models, kindling my path to self-healing. They opened the doorway to an endless hallway of doors.

CHAPTER 5

February 1990
1 Month Old

J oyce secured a short-term placement in a halfway house after my stay at Clare's Well. I'd been clean for months, but she worried I was at risk of a relapse since I no longer had the incentive of pregnancy. She also thought I would benefit from a safe and structured environment.

I went back to work at the camera shop, grateful to have a steady paycheck, and attended Narcotics Anonymous meetings regularly. During my pregnancy, I'd developed new coping skills that didn't include drugs or alcohol, and even though I still wanted to avoid my feelings, at least I wasn't using chemicals to do so. Through NA, the people I met were young, energetic, and committed to improving their lives, and I threw myself into social events. In April, I moved into an apartment with two of them.

I attended a monthly first parent's support group with Joyce. I did not grasp how lucky I was: like the option for choosing open adoption, the inclusion of a support group after relinquishment was a new component in the world of adoption.

I wanted to move on with my life, but anxiety about my baby, about *Michael*, dominated my thoughts. That, and the upcoming face-to-face with the adoptive parents, stood like a barricade between the past and future. I had their file, which included the letters and portrait photos, but I wanted to know what they looked like in real life: to see how they interacted with each other and to hear their voices. I needed to get a sense of how they took up space — to get a three-dimensional image.

In hopes it might help aid my grief process, Joyce asked the adoptive family to meet me before the final court date. Adoptive parents, she said, often feared the first parent would try to take the baby back and may not agree, but Joyce assured them I was confident of my decision.

When I arrived at the adoption agency, the family was already there. Joyce ushered me into a tiny conference room where light from the overhead fixture bathed the space in a soft glow: small oakwood table, conference chairs upholstered in peach, framed art matted in lavender—all soft, calming pastels.

"This is Jane and David, and the little guy is John," Joyce said, closing the door behind us.

"Hi Candace," David stood. His torso blocked out the window behind him; he reminded me of a football player. He extended a meaty hand, which I awkwardly shook, and then took a seat. Jane remained seated quietly. Her coifed brown hair and thick, large-rimmed glasses completely over-powered her tiny frame.

Abruptly, John leaped onto one of the chairs, shot his arms up in the air, and yelled, "I'm gonna be four!" His spikey blond hair mirrored his upstretched arms, and dimples dotted his cheeks.

I couldn't help but smile.

Although Michael had been with them since early February, he was not present. Joyce had suggested, and I agreed, it might be too hard to see him. Plus, Joyce did not think they would have agreed to this meeting if asked to bring Michael.

"I just want to say it's wonderful to meet you." David smiled. Tears brimmed in his pale blue eyes; his cropped blond hair framed a round face. Using both his hands, he clasped one of Jane's tiny hands and cradled it in his lap.

He told me about the excitement Michael's arrival had created in their small town and how friends and family continued to come by daily with gifts and well wishes. David handed me a picture of Michael taken the previous week, and I noticed the absence of the tiny pimples and newborn wrinkles. I tore my eyes away from it and set it on the small conference table; I did not want to be rude by ignoring them. I also didn't want to damage it with my sweaty hands.

John was a welcome diversion until he settled down on the carpeted floor with crayons. Throughout our discussion, I watched the interactions between him and David closely. Based on what I could see, Michael was already getting more than I could ever give him. My chest tightened. *I may not have what Michael needs to thrive, but David clearly does.*

I tried to present a brave front, but tears snuck out in fits and starts.

David wept almost non-stop, and at one point, John paused in his coloring. "My dad cries all the time," he said, his tone light-hearted and matter of fact, "but they are tears of joy."

I took a slow breath, and my shoulders relaxed. Knowing that David was unashamed to express his feelings and share them with John gave me a sense of solace I hadn't anticipated. Prior to this meeting, I believed they would fulfill Michael's needs for physical comfort and monetary stability, but now I knew it would not be at the expense of love and compassion. This man would assume the mantle of fatherhood and do it justice. He would be a caregiver, disciplinarian, and breadwinner. He would teach my son, *our son*, how to make his way in the world confidently and bravely, without the need to step on anyone else. He would show my son compassion, self-confidence, and courage.

After this single meeting, David became my hero.

Jane, on the other hand, remained quiet and unobtrusive. Perhaps she was purposefully trying to blend into the background, or maybe she was used to David taking the reins. Maybe she was unhappy to be there. For whatever reason, I gave her little attention. It may have been as simple as not wanting to acknowledge the other mother – for both of us.

"We agree to send an update at six months," David said, "another at one year, and one every year after that."

"Please mail them to us at this address," Joyce handed David a card, "and we will forward them. Candace, you can send updates in return, if you choose," she gave me a card too. "Okay, that just leaves one more item," she said, directing her comments to David and Jane. "Candace has decided to keep her file open here at the agency, so when Michael turns eighteen, if he chooses, he can find her."

I nodded, then softly added, "Yes." But what I didn't tell them, or anyone else for years, was that I never expected to see him again.

When I walked out of the conference room, I told myself this was the end. Having met the family and found them worthy, I would now close this chapter of my life. I'd permitted myself to grieve his loss at Helen's and Clare's Well, so that was it. I would move on.

But in a tiny part of my heart, tucked away in the bottom of a drawer, wrapped in a blue baby blanket, an ember of hope glowed. I wouldn't fan it, but I couldn't douse it either. Hope that in the future, he'd want to meet me. Hope for a phone call—or a letter. Somehow, someday, I prayed he'd want to know me. But along with that hope came fear, which forced me to recoil as if it were a snake or scorpion. A fear harbored in my soul that consumed me at times: that he would hate me for giving him away.

CHAPTER 6

August 1990
7 Months Old

I stood on the porch flipping through a pile of bills when I spotted the non-descript white envelope. My heart stalled. It had the adoption agency's return address.

It was the beginning of August, and this had to be the first update. I resisted the urge to tear it open on the spot. I wanted to savor the experience, and I needed privacy.

I took the stairs three at a time up to our third-floor apartment and barreled past the kitchen, breathing hard. I ignored my roommates, watching TV, and went to my room. Locking the door, I collapsed cross-legged onto the floor. Heartbeats thundered in my chest. Slipping my forefinger under one side of the envelope flap, I gently pulled up, careful to preserve its integrity. Inside was a three-page handwritten letter on lined notebook paper wrapped around an assortment of photos.

I examined each photo before I placed it on the matted shag carpet. I meticulously spaced and balanced them symmetrically: three horizontal images in the middle, one vertical on each end, and a vertical portrait below. Then, I unfolded the letter.

Beautiful writing flowed across the page, a blend of cursive and printed words, but not David's. *This must be Jane's penmanship.*

July 27, 1990
Dear Candace,
Sorry this is a little late, but we had some problems with our

camera. John was pretending he was taking a picture and acciden-tally dropped it. As he did that, the back of the camera popped open, and the almost used up film got exposed, and the flash broke! Long story, huh? So, then we borrowed our niece's camera and took a whole roll of pictures again. So anyway, enclosed is a six-month-old picture of Michael.

Well, I guess I'll forgive you for being late.

Michael has changed so much since we met with you. For one thing, he has lost a lot of that beautiful red hair.

I looked at the close-up of Michael. Blond fuzz like an aura was just visible on the top of his head. I sighed.

He does have some hair, but it has really lightened up. We are hoping that it will turn red again. It does have a slight reddish tint to it, though. Everyone that has seen John and Michael together tells us how close they resemble each other. Especially with the light hair and fair complexion.

Smiling, I grabbed a three-by-five snapshot of John awkwardly cradling Michael. How lucky to have two adopted boys with such strikingly similar features.

Michael is creeping along the floor now and can get to about anything he wants to, including John's toys! John is very patient and doesn't get too upset when he gets into his things.

At four-and-a-half months, Michael cut his first tooth and now has two teeth on the bottom. He is a very content and happy baby. He is so smiley, and when he gets excited, he screams out with laughter. He also has a little temper which he doesn't use too often, mostly when he wants his bottle. When he wants it, he wants it <u>now</u>!

My mind played out the scene, imagining his face beet-red and fists flailing.

When I had Michael to the doctor, he weighed almost eighteen pounds. He is really filling out. He is starting to get little rolls on his arms and legs.

I chuckled at the pudgy fat under Michael's chin in another photo.

Michael thoroughly enjoys eating. He has been a healthy baby. We've only had to take him to the doctor for his checkups. He's had a few colds but nothing serious.
We feel so blessed and are so thankful to have such beautiful children. John loves Michael so much. It is also fun for John to watch Michael grow up and do different things. He gets as excited as we do when Michael does something new. Also, Michael totally adores John. He gets so excited when he wakes up and sees John or whenever John talks to him. John thinks that's pretty neat too.

Remembering John's chattiness, I envisioned playful interactions between the two boys.

We are hoping and praying that all is going well for you, Candace. We think of you often and hope that everything is working out for the best. We are glad that we were able to meet you. Afterward, John said, "I really liked that lady."

I grinned. *I liked you too, John.*

We want you to know that you should never worry about Michael. He could never be more loved and cared for. They are both so special. We thank God every day for them. God bless you.
David and Jane.
P.S. We will send another picture and update in six months.

Tears of solemn happiness trickled down my face. I reread the letter twice, then folded it up, matching the creases exactly. These were just the kinds of details I'd hoped they would include. I reexamined all the photos multiple times, smiling through tears, then slid them into the envelope with the letter. Then, I placed everything in the bottom right-hand drawer of my dresser, which already held

Michael's hospital bracelet, first pacifier, and the blue baby blanket he'd last used at the hospital—the one I'd stolen.

Despite the counseling I'd received, I didn't know how to navigate the intense emotions related to Michael, or any feelings for that matter. My default was to block, deny, or mask feelings. And I thought maybe I wouldn't drown if I could restrict them within a defined framework. So, this routine became ritual-like in its solemnity—sitting on my bedroom floor, alone, wherever I happened to live, devouring the contents of each new update. Then, I'd pull out the previous updates and incorporate all the photos into my painstakingly crafted pattern. On the days I'd felt strong and resolute, I reread all the letters, but sometimes I could only bear to look at the pictures.

Viewing the photos gave me a sense of security and comfort in the lives they were building together. A fullness. Visual confirmation of things I never had and never could give, and proof I'd chosen wisely. And no matter how much time passed, I craved assurance that Michael was safe, so I performed the photo montage ritual on other days too. His birthday. Mother's Day. Anytime I needed a reminder that he was okay. During the first couple of years, I laid out the photos and read the letters every couple of weeks; then slowly, as if a scab had grown over a wound, I picked at it less and less. But every time I finished laying out the photo collage and rereading the letters, I pulled out his blue baby blanket, lifted it to my face, and inhaled. The grief would start in the back of my throat and burst to the surface, spewing forth in a torrent.

Over the years, my tears washed away Michael's scent until only the smell of sadness remained.

CHAPTER 7

Fall 1990
8 Months Old

Ihad turned twenty-two in July, was healthy and ambitious. If Michael did decide to find me one day, I wanted him to see I hadn't squandered the opportunity, so I applied to St. Cloud State University. I latched onto the idea with a mixture of enthusiasm and desperation; I knew education and a respectable job would benefit me but also welcomed the distraction.

"I got in!" I yelled as I burst through the apartment door, waving my acceptance letter in the air. My two roommates sat at the kitchen table playing cribbage.

"You go, girl," Sharon grabbed a handful of M&M's from a bowl in the middle of the table and plopped them into her mouth. "I'll show you around campus if you want," she said between crunches.

I loved my roommates and our three-bedroom apartment. The flat sprawled across the entire third floor of an early nineteenth-century brick house, complete with climbing vines and a wraparound porch. Acquaintances from NA dropped by often, filling the space with laughter and friendship; I'd never experienced such ease or support in my living space. For the first time in my life, I felt mature and focused on the right path.

Once school began, I applied myself with rigor and dedication. I studied every day and acquired a work-study position on campus in addition to working at the camera shop. I had continued attending the first mother's support group sporadically through the summer, at

Joyce's urging, but as my energy shifted to campus life, I eventually withdrew from the agency's support systems. I didn't want to remind myself of my child's absence and instead chose to fill the hole with busyness and diversions.

Then, I met Grant.

The brother of a co-worker, he picked me up for our blind date in a late model Chrysler New Yorker town car. Black. Sleek. Elegant. His long limbs, wispy black hair, and hawk-like nose made me think of Ichabod Crane, but I ignored that when Grant held the front gate for me and opened the car door like a real gentleman. We went out to dinner, a movie, and at the end of the evening, he walked me to my door; no demands, no kiss, just courteous distance.

Over the following year, we went out almost every Friday night. He wrote me weekly love letters on light blue stationery, and once a month, he brought me flowers for no reason. No one had ever bought me flowers before. And when we became sexually intimate, he didn't hesitate to use a condom. Grant was respectful, responsible, and a successful independent contractor – a good catch.

After almost a year of dating, we moved in together. Grant insisted he have his own room, which I thought was odd, but he wanted some separation in case things didn't work out. We delegated household chores, maintained separate finances, ate dinner together, and fell into an easy domestic partnership. And on Friday nights, we shared a bed.

I liked the privacy and the space. It enabled me to keep to myself whenever I felt vulnerable. Although Grant knew about Michael, he never knew I cried alone sometimes, reliving the grief and loss of my child. When updates arrived, I relished the semblance of intimacy I gleaned from them, then squirreled them away.

After moving in with Grant, I began volunteering at the Central Minnesota Sexual Assault Center (CMSAC) as a victim advocate. The work was intense, painful, and freeing. This role, along with my experience through an unplanned pregnancy, would shape the direction of my studies.

I loved college, and the more time I spent with people dedicated to improving their lives, the healthier and happier I became. I finally settled on a major, Social Work, which is when I met Steph.

She'd walked assertively up to me after an Introduction to Social Work class, introduced herself, and invited me for coffee. Tall and bigboned, with long, permed hair sprayed into a voluminous crown, she radiated self-confidence. She didn't actually drink coffee, so got a Mountain Dew from the cafeteria vending machine, and then we talked as if we'd been friends since childhood.

I discovered her confidence was part façade, used to keep people at arm's length, but she'd welcomed me in, and I returned the favor by opening up about topics I'd rarely told anyone else.

"I'm already learning so much about myself and my family in these classes. It's kind of eye-opening and a bit scary." She cracked open a third can of soda.

"Yeah, families can be scary, that's for sure," I said, brows furrowed. The light outside had dimmed with the waning day. "I've got kind of a tough background."

"Wanna share?" She leaned forward.

Surprised, I realized I *did* want to share with her. "Sexual abuse. My stepdad. Until I was thirteen."

"Whoa, I'm sorry," her forehead creased dramatically.

"Well, it's over now and," I returned her unwavering eye contact and smiled, "I'm okay." And for the first time, I believed what I said. My training with the CMSAC, including counseling and a support group, along with not using drugs to self-medicate, allowed me to work through my feelings. Perhaps most importantly, I learned the value of talking with other survivors.

"I'm glad," she said and reached over to touch my arm. Then, Steph proceeded to fill me in on her dad, who she adored, her mom, who she described as overbearing, and her older brother. "I'm just realizing that he has undiagnosed Asperger's. I couldn't ever figure out why he acted so aloof and why, at thirty years of age, he still lives at home."

Although our experiences differed, mutual compassion formed a solid foundation for friendship.

We navigated the Social Work Department side by side for the next two years, her focus on veterans' mental health, while mine was child abuse and sexual violence. On Saturday nights, she and I drove to out-in-the-sticks dive bars to listen to live rock-n-roll and dance the night away.

At some point, after I met Steph, Grant proposed. I placed the one-carat engagement ring proudly on my finger: a symbol of middle-class prosperity and upward mobility. But I wasn't in any hurry to marry—obtaining my degree was the priority. So, we agreed to wait to wed until after I graduated and got a job.

Shortly before graduation, I learned the CMSAC director had written a grant for a new full-time position.

"Do you know what the job description is yet?" Steph threw her long hair over her shoulder, then took a slug off her Mountain Dew. The Brick Yard where we typically had lunch buzzed with conversations.

"Responsibility for developing and implementing educational sexual abuse prevention programming in the four-county area. High schools, grade schools, police departments, you name it." I leaned in over the table. "Also, expanded outreach in the outlying counties, and, of course, direct client services for victims and their families."

"It's perfect for you!" The corners of her mouth curved widely. "You've got solid public speaking experience, have already been through the advocacy training program, and you're about to graduate. You just need to tweak your resume." I could hardly believe it: my dream job. But, I had to wait to see if it would come to fruition.

In the spring of 1994, I graduated with a BS in Social Work, magna cum laude. I'd written grants and received scholarships during the last two years of school, in addition to working, so by the time I graduated, I was less than one thousand dollars in debt. Pride in my accomplishments and excitement filled my chest as I received my diploma; I didn't even care that none of my family came to witness. And as icing on the cake, the university presented me with an Excellence in Leadership award for outstanding campus achievement.

While I waited for the CMSAC position to open, I sent my resume to just one other place: Caritas Family Services. They had an opening for a crisis pregnancy counselor—Joyce's position; she'd been promoted.

In the end, I was offered both jobs but was delighted to accept the Multi-County Coordinator position just two months after graduation.

My first salaried job.

I was on my way.

CHAPTER 8

After I settled into my new job, Grant and I took the next step in our relationship: we bought a house together. It seemed the logical step along the road to success. Our discussions regarding house types, number of bedrooms and bathrooms, and how much acreage to consider morphed into divvying up chores and financial responsibilities.

When I first met Grant, I considered him a "good catch." Purchasing property was proof of that. The fact that we still didn't share a bedroom, even in the new house with its glorious master suite, didn't faze me. There'd never been much chemistry between us. Currently, we were intimate once a week, like clockwork.

I figured romantic love was overrated.

CHAPTER 9

November 1995
5 Years Old

❝Tom! Is that you?" I recognized his voice immediately. He'd called me a couple of times since that day we sat together in the basement of my mom's house. His kindness had been imprinted in my mind.

"Yep. It's me. Surprise! I'm in town, wanna have lunch?"

Even though I knew he couldn't see me over the phone, I smiled and readily agreed.

The next day, he leaned against the wrought iron fence surrounding the restaurant entrance, arm draped over a finial, his breath visible as little white puffs. We embraced longer than expected, but not so long as to become awkward.

"It's so good to see you!" I said, noting scents of soap and tobacco that clung to his jacket. "I can't believe it's been five years!"

The hostess escorted us to a high back booth on the second floor. The warm scent of fresh popovers floated around the spacious dining room and mingled with fond memories of Tom.

I slid onto the bench seat, opened the menu, and peeked over the top. His hair was long enough that he had it pulled back in a ponytail; tiny curls escaped at his temples.

I always loved those natural curls.

"I'm living in Texas now, working for Schlumberger as an engineering specialist. I just came back to Minnesota to go hunting. I'm staying with my friend, Joe, and was trying to help by doing dishes. Stuck my hand in a glass and, bang, it shattered." He held up a bandaged hand.

His easy smile and conversational tone transported me back into our old friendship.

"So, I figured I might as well reconnect!"

"Why aren't you staying with your folks?"

"They moved down to Arizona. They love it. But, hey, how are you?"

"I'm good." I propped my chin up with one hand. "I've been working at the Sexual Assault Center for over a year now, mostly providing community education. I love it. I mean, it's hard, for sure, but it's powerful work, important work. I just finished conducting a sensitivity workshop at the sheriff's department this morning, and tomorrow I'll be presenting a healthy sexuality class at Apollo High School—your alma mater."

We continued talking about our jobs for a while, voices lively, arms animated until I finally asked if he was dating anyone.

"Naw, I haven't seen anyone since my trip to Australia."

He launched into an account of a bicycle trip he took two years before. A year-long tour of North America that morphed into an inter-continental adventure, including the U.S., Mexico, Fiji, Tahiti, Hawaii, Australia, and New Zealand. As he eagerly recounted his experiences in the Outback and rescuing an injured falcon, I felt an old stirring.

My pulse increased, accompanied by a flutter in my belly.

"Oh my God, that's amazing! I've never thought about doing anything so adventurous." *And brave. And daring. Whoa, am I responding to his story or him?*

"So, what about you? Are you still seeing Grant?"

"Yeah, we just bought a house together out in St. Joe. And we're engaged," I felt blood rush to my cheeks. I held up my left hand, palm facing me, and wiggled my fingers to draw attention to my engagement ring. "We haven't set a date or anything, but probably in the next year or so." I put my hands down in my lap and twisted the ring under the table. "I guess we're waiting to get settled into the house."

Tom visibly paled, and his eyes bulged. "Wow. I didn't realize you guys were so serious." His gaze lowered, and he pushed his salad around with his fork, then set it aside without taking a bite. "Shit."

"What?"

"I gotta tell you something."

My head lifted slightly, eyebrows raised.

Another longish pause. "I, uh, I'm not sure how to say this, but… I love you."

I sat back, knocking my head against the high-backed booth, my hand instinctively raised to cradle my head. Tom continued.

"I've loved you since we first met."

I dropped my hand and gaped at him.

"And I just realized, this very moment, that if I don't tell you now, I'm going to regret it." He leaned back in the booth, held my gaze for a moment, and then averted his eyes. A painfully long pause ensued.

Looking up again, he continued, "Back when we were first hanging out, I had a girlfriend. And since then, you've been in a relationship. But now, I guess I need to tell you. That's it."

Butterflies buzzed in my stomach, and I flushed and looked away. My palms were suddenly sweaty. "I loved you too," I whispered, a tingling sensation between my shoulder blades. "We had a great connection back in high school, but… I'm engaged now." My hands, of their own accord, wrung in my lap. "And… I just bought a house…" as if that would be the end of it.

Abruptly, I stood. "Ah, it was good to see you, but I need to get back to work." I crumpled my napkin, dropped it on my plate, and bolted. Once I reached the sidewalk, I slowed and tried to get a grasp on the uneasiness creeping under my skin.

Tom? Do I still have feelings for Tom?

I'd been with Grant for three years. We had a house—season tickets to the theatre. We had just vacationed in Disneyland. And we were going to get married. Our life together was taking the shape of the American Dream.

So why did I suddenly feel off-balance? Light-headed? Like an electrical current was coursing up and down my spine?

It was uncomfortable, yet, invigorating too.

What the hell was going on?

"Hey, Candy!" Tom called, running to catch up to me. "Do you want to go play pool tonight at the Red Carpet?"

"Um," with no time to think and unable to come up with a reason not to, I said, "Yeah. Sure." The hair on my arms bristled with more than excitement. "Can I bring a friend?"

"Absolutely!"

We made hurried arrangements, and when I got back to work, I called Steph.

"Hey, so, um, are you free tonight?"

"Yeah," she paused. "What's wrong?"

"Nothing. I don't know. Well... Do you remember me telling you about my friend, Tom, from high school?"

"Vaguely."

"Well, I just had lunch with him." I gave her an abbreviated synopsis of our last-minute lunch date and his unexpected declaration of love.

"Holy shit! Do you still have feelings for him?" Her voice rose with excitement.

"No. Yeah. Oh my god, I don't know. My heart is beating like a hundred miles an hour."

"All right, take a deep breath. Meet me at my place beforehand so we can talk, then we'll go together."

Distracted and alarmed at my churning emotions, I left work early. On the drive home, I realized I'd never felt this surge of electricity—this kind of desire—as if a current zipped through my veins. I was drawn to the intensity but frightened at the same time.

I pulled up to the house and stopped at the end of the short drive, my stomach roiling. The sky had turned gray and cast a pall over the yard. Patches of green covered the five-acre lawn, hanging on despite several hard freezes. The weeping willow tree I'd planted after moving in waved its straggling limbs forlornly in the breeze. I wasn't sure it would survive the winter.

Plans for a half-acre vegetable garden adjacent to the basement patio and a lattice-covered gazebo out back seemed stupid and meaningless. I didn't even know if I liked gardening. I shook my head and pulled into the garage.

The sparse furnishings and blank walls accentuated the feeling of careening from room to room like a rubber ball as I killed time until I knew Steph would be home. I scribbled a quick note to Grant, anchoring it to the counter with the peppermill, then gratefully backed out the drive.

"I'd like you to be a buffer," I said to Steph twenty minutes later, after sharing the chaos going on inside my head. "I'm just... I'm worried I'm going to do something foolish."

"Like what?"

"I don't know. That's why I need you. Just give me a shove, or something, if I'm acting dumb."

She smacked me on the arm.

"Ha. Ha. Very funny."

"Don't worry, I've got your back," she pulled me in for a hug. Steph's full, soft, lingering hugs never felt hurried, intrusive, or obligatory.

That night, Steph joked with Tom like an old friend, teasing him about his mediocre pool playing and poor dart shots while he flirted back, trying to impress her with compliments. Steph helped keep the mood light and friendly, and an easy camaraderie sprung up between the three of us. At the end of the evening, I surprised myself when I invited them over for dinner the next night.

I slept little that night, alone in the brand-new, queen-size, four-poster cherry wood bed. I don't remember if Grant was home; his bedroom and office were downstairs.

Questions swirled around in my head. *What were these feelings about Tom? Did those feelings impact how I felt about Grant? How* ***did*** *I feel about Grant? Was I happy with Grant? If I was happy, why was I thinking about Tom?*

Back-to-back high school health classes provided the perfect distraction the next day, requiring my focused concentration on the presentations. Early that evening, Steph arrived with Tom, who she'd picked up on her way to my house. We talked over each other excitedly, the aroma of sautéed garlic and onions, and the sound of Steph's unmistakable bark-like laughter blended and resonated off the vaulted ceiling. Tom's allergies flared up, his watering eyes and sneezes brought on by Batman, my yellow-eyed, midnight-black cat.

Grant arrived and sat at the head of the table just as the lasagna came out of the oven. After introducing Tom as an old friend, he dominated the conversation with tales of his traveling exploits. Tom held eye contact for long moments, speaking with animated enthusiasm, as both Steph and I leaned in eagerly, then reeled back with thunderous laughter.

An oppressive silence descended after Steph and Tom left, which I rushed to fill with clanging pots and pans and the roar of the dishwasher. Later, as I slipped into bed, I heard Grant on the stairs then his slow steps in the hall.

He stopped at the doorway to the master bedroom, silhouetted against the hallway light. "I can't believe you invited someone to dinner who is so clearly in love with you."

I couldn't see his facial expression, but I waited to see what else he would say.

Nothing.

What did I expect? Did I want him to sit down and have a heart-to-heart with me? Tell me he loved me? Fight for me?

When he didn't say anything else, I switched on my alarm clock, then rolled over and gave him my back. After I heard his departing footsteps, barely detectable on the carpet, I shifted onto my back and stared at the ceiling.

Frustrated with inertia and paralysis, I flicked on the light and grabbed my journal from the nightstand, my go-to tool to ease anxiety, find clarity, and get unstuck. After the initial vomit of free-written words, I settled into a writing rhythm and let my thoughts flow onto the page.

Early the following day, Grant returned to my bedroom, lifted the comforter, and slipped into bed. Scooching over, he reached around my waist to spoon, his breath hot on my neck. I lay for mere moments, heat rushing into my extremities, before throwing the covers off and lurching out of bed.

"Suddenly, you have the desire to talk to me, to be with me?" My voice sizzled. "It's too little, Grant. Too little, too late." I stalked into the bathroom and locked the door. I faced the mirror, hands on the edge of the counter, elbows locked. I glared at my reflection. My arms began to shake. Who was this woman staring back at me, and what did she want?

I was angry, but at who? Grant for not trying harder to win me over or at myself for not asking for more—for setting the bar so low?

When I emerged from the bathroom, Grant was gone.

I packed a few things and drove to Steph's. I spent the next several evenings sleeping on an inflatable mattress in her living room, journaling and hashing out with her what was going on in my head.

"Do you and Grant still maintain separate finances?" Steph asked as she grabbed a deck of cards and held them up to me, eyebrows raised. "Wanna play?" She never missed an opportunity to play cards.

I nodded. "I'm paying the mortgage while he covers utilities and miscellaneous expenses."

"Hum." She shuffled the cards, then dealt as she spoke. "You guys hardly ever spend time together on weekends. It seems like he's always doing something with his brother, hunting or trap shooting. And he never comes to Sharon and Leslie's or any of our friends' parties, either."

"You're right. He doesn't."

"What about bookstores? Do you ever go together?"

I barked. "Yeah, right. Grant at a feminist bookstore?"

"I didn't think so. You know, I always thought it was weird that he didn't come to your graduation. That was a big deal."

"Well, he had to work."

"And you always let him off easy," she sighed, her eyes focused on the cards fanned out in front of her. Then she reminded me of the time I'd gone to the Mayo Clinic to have a suspicious lump removed from my breast and how he hadn't offered to accompany me.

"Does he ever ask you about Michael?"

"No."

"Do you talk to him about Michael? Share the updates with him?"

"No."

"Why not?"

"I don't know." I shrugged. "It's private."

Steph frowned; her head tilted forward.

The slap of cards and tick of the clock echoed off the sliding glass patio doors.

"You know, I don't think I've ever seen you two hold hands," she peeked over her cards.

We didn't. I couldn't think of a single time we'd walked hand in hand. We didn't cuddle on the couch watching movies or snuggle in bed.

"Have you ever considered that you're with Grant because he doesn't demand your actual participation?"

Her comment felt like a slap in the face. The good kind. The wake-up kind.

I didn't have to do anything, and neither did he, but we reaped the benefits of being in a relationship. Grant was building his American Dream, and I wondered for the first time if *his* dream was truly *my* dream.

No. It wasn't. And I was just figuring that out.

So, what *did* I want?

Love. I want love. And passion. And compassion.

Tom's declaration of love had cracked open my heart. I was terrified and fascinated at the thought. *Is this love? What does love even feel like? I don't know, but whatever this is, I want more.* I'd kept my emotions locked up and inaccessible because they always seemed to cause distress, but now, the things I was feeling were electric, delightful, magical, and for once, I found myself *wanting* to feel. And, with my increased self-esteem and confidence, I began to consider that perhaps I deserve love too. And if this was love, which I thought it was, I wanted to welcome it and not turn it away.

Resting on the blow-up mattress in Steph's living room a couple of days later, I listened to Pink Floyd's "Breathe" on my Walkman. The waves of the instrumental introduction swelled through the headphones into the opening lyrics, and I caught my breath:

Breathe, breathe in the air

Don't be afraid to care

Leave, don't leave me

Look around, choose your own ground.

Less than a week later, I met Grant at a downtown restaurant. Slushy snow had turned into a frozen pond near the entrance, and he hugged me stiffly before placing his hand on my lower back to guide me inside.

"Well, what are we going to do?" he asked as soon as we took our seats.

"I want to end our engagement," I said quickly, like pulling off a Band-aid. "I deserve a true mate, not a business partner." I held his gaze. "We both do."

He sighed, and his shoulders slumped in defeat.

The remainder of our discussion consisted primarily of apologies—on both sides. In the end, Grant agreed to leave the house so I could move back in and put it on the market.

Five weeks later, I called Tom.

"Hey," my heart beat staccato in my chest. "This is Candace."

"Hiiiiiii." The word strung out, pitch rising in the middle.

"Hey, I, um, just wanted to call and, um, let you know Grant and I broke up."

"Really? Are you okay? What happened?"

"Well, I just decided I wasn't really into the house, two-point-five kids, American Dream thing, I guess. I've got the property up for sale and am looking for an apartment."

"Whoa, wow." A short silence followed by a deep intake of breath. "I didn't expect to hear from you again."

Did I hear excitement in his tone of voice? "I know, but," I swallowed. "I want more. Grant understands. We parted amicably, for the most part." I paused, unsure what I wanted to say or how to say it. *How does one go about consciously starting a relationship?*

Tom was quiet on the other end of the line.

"You said you loved me," I blurted, "and now I'm single, and I thought, well, maybe you'd be interested in exploring that a little?" Leaning forward, grasping the phone tightly, I hardly breathed.

CHAPTER 10

February 1996
6 Years Old

No update arrived in the mail the year Michael turned six. But with the chaos of selling the house and my budding relationship with Tom, I didn't obsess about it and didn't contact the agency until mid-February. When I did, the new caseworker agreed to forward a reminder to the adoptive family in the form of a polite request, and I settled back to wait.

I'd rented the perfect apartment in a folk Victorian house, walking distance from downtown, with dusty wood trim and creaky floors. I loved the nooks and crannies, especially the old-fashioned laundry chute with its cracked porcelain knob, permanently closed by a single rusty nail. The apartment was the opposite of the sterile, colorless modern house I'd shared with Grant, offering another clear example of our incompatibility.

In March, the update finally arrived. The single-page letter apologized for being tardy. There seemed to be less depth to it, almost a rational quality: Michael's family life was hectic but happy; he was hitting all his developmental marks and growing into a fine young man. I snorted.

He's still just a little boy.

Amongst the photos was a pretend trading card of Michael dressed in his little league uniform, poised at-bat. Sky blue eyes with whisper-light lashes peeked from beneath his dark blue ball cap. A grin stretched from ear to ear. "Little Slugger," it proclaimed, with his "stats" on the back. I shook my head in wonder. I'd never seen anything like it. In our family, we'd always scraped by to get the no-frills, value-pack of school pictures, the kind that fit as many images on a single page as possible.

In the spring, Tom quit his job in Texas, drove back to Minnesota towing a U-Haul trailer, and moved seamlessly in with me. We bumped into each other playfully in the evenings while concocting elaborate meals, which we ate by candlelight. My favorite was sautéed jumbo shrimp bathed in a rich, silky cream sauce that he licked off my fingers. And from the beginning of our romantic relationship, Tom's gentle attentions and clear desire for a mutually satisfying love life put me at ease. He respected my boundaries and helped me learn to trust my body. He made intimacy not only safe but enjoyable for the first time in my life.

I thought this might be domestic bliss.

One night, after dinner, we'd just settled on the couch to watch *Third Rock from the Sun* when he asked, "Would you like to go on an extended bike trip?"

I vaulted to an upright position on the edge of the couch. "Absolutely! But do you think I could do it?"

"Of course. It's not like it's hard; it's just peddling." He laughed and turned to face me. "We'd have to sell your Accord and put all our stuff in storage, but I was crunching some numbers, and with the money from the car combined with my savings, I think we could go for a whole year."

"Holy crap, really?" I could feel my pulse in my throat. He'd clearly given the idea considerable thought. "What about my job?"

"Well, aren't you ready for a break? I mean, you've talked about feeling run down a lot lately. You haven't seemed all that excited to get up and go to work since I moved in."

He was right. I dreaded going into the office. Although I loved the educational and public speaking aspects of my job, the one-on-one counseling had drained me to the point of exhaustion. I knew what this was, and so did the agency director: burn-out. A common fate in my line of work, I'd just figured it would never happen to me.

"You know, there's nothing wrong with taking a year or two off. When I got back from my bike trip, the company hired me back right away. Not that it would be the same for you, but I know I was more enthusiastic for the job when I went back."

"Where would we go?" Already, dreams of exotic, far-away locations sprang to mind.

"From here, I thought we'd follow the Mississippi River down to southern Tennessee, cut west through Texas, and drop down into Mexico," his hands traced a line in the air as his voice rose with excitement. "Then, I'd like to keep going south, cross the Panama Canal, and go all the way to Tierra del Fuego, Argentina, then head back north and finish the year in Alaska!"

I'd never dreamed of doing something so daring. So big. Yet it seemed…logical, an obvious step in my evolution to independence, confidence, and tenacity. It could provide a clean break from the bonds of expectations—my own and others'—where I could exist outside the confines of the past. And, someday, if Michael ever found me, what a story I'd be able to tell.

In June, I resigned from my position at the Sexual Assault Center and picked up a less stressful job at a local coffee shop while Tom researched routes, bikes, and gear. Little slips of paper littered the apartment, scrawled with tidbits of travel information and reminders in his atrocious handwriting. I bought a brand-new bike, my first, a Raleigh M400, and for my birthday, Tom gave me clip-in shoes, cycling tights, and tandem rims.

We departed on our "Tour of the Americas" on October 1, 1996, biking to my mom's house on the way out of town. Since Michael's adoption, I seldom saw or spoke to Mom. I tried to be cordial when I did, and we never talked about him. I'd informed her that I would be leaving on an extended bicycle trip back in July, and she'd agreed to host a going-away party.

Tom and I enthusiastically pulled out our map and laid it on the table, tracing our route for everyone to see. My siblings smiled and nodded, crowding around, but Mom putzed around the kitchen and seemed entirely disinterested. So, after a piece of cake, we said our goodbyes and slipped away.

Outside her split-level home, we doubled checked the bulky packs which protruded from both front and back racks. Fully loaded, Tom's bike weighed one-hundred-ten pounds; mine ninety-seven. I stood proudly on the driveway, smiling girlishly, unable to contain my excitement.

"Well," Mom said from the front step, "aren't those something?" But her tone and accompanying frown indicated she *didn't* think they were something at all. Dried yellow leaves littered the yard and crunched underfoot on her approach; the moist scent of decay lingered in the cool air.

My girlish smile faded, and I shrugged. Even though I was thrilled at what was to come, I knew there would be no pleasing Mom.

"Hey, I'm gonna use the bathroom one more time," I said to Tom, leaving him with Mom.

When I returned, my indifferent emotional barrier firmly back in place, I hugged Mom and said, "I'll call once a month or so to let you know I'm okay."

"You're sure you want to do this?" She gripped my upper arms, face pinched like she'd just eaten a lemon.

"Yes, Mom, I am. I'll be all right. I love you."

"I love you too, honey." Her response seemed even more robotic than mine.

About five miles out of town, when we stopped for a break, Tom shared what Mom said to him while I was in the house. She'd bee-lined over to him, and jabbing a finger into his chest, accused him of ruining my life. According to her, he was leading me to my death, and she would never forgive him.

"Holy crap, really?"

"Yes. I just stood there. What could I say?"

"Nothing, I guess." I shook my head, incredulous, but knowing in my heart, it was true. "You know I don't believe that, right? You know I am thrilled to be on this adventure with you?"

"Yes, I *do* know that," he said confidently, "but what about your mom? Are *you* okay?"

"Tom, Mom is Mom." I sighed. "I think that maybe she's jealous? Or mad that I'm doing something she can't. Whatever happens, she never seems happy. I know she'll never approve of anyone I'm with, just like she's not happy with Stacy and Miles's choices." I shook my head. "I can't win when it comes to Mom, and I'm not going to try anymore because it just makes me feel bad. And, I finally realize, I don't want to feel bad." A bright ray of sun broke through the clouds, illuminating the road before us. "I am embarking on this trip with my eyes wide open, probably for the first time in my life."

The weather turned cold within the week, but the physical exertion kept us warm during the day, and our new, zip-together sleeping bags kept us cozy at night. We played scrabble by flashlight before bed, and by the time we got to Mexico, we'd adjusted to tent living, showering at campgrounds, cooking on a WhisperLite stove, and traveling fifty-sixty miles a day.

Although we always had a distance or destination goal, our pace was unhurried. We would stop whenever we wanted and stay as long as we liked. We met all kinds of people who invited us into their homes to share a meal and conversation. And even in Mexico, despite our broken Spanish and outdated dictionary, we were welcomed with curiosity and warmth.

Just before Christmas, we biked to Edzna, a little-known Mayan Ruin outside the city of Campeche. The thirty-five-mile ride over cracked asphalt roads ended at a gravel parking lot, almost deserted but for three travel-dusted cars. We leaned our bikes against a giant Ceiba tree, and as I drained a water bottle, I glimpsed an edge of slate-grey stone above the tree canopy, like a castle fortress.

We explored the ruins together and marveled at the giant staircases and elaborate rainwater collection system. We didn't have a blanket, so Tom spread one of our towels in the shade at the edge of the beautifully manicured central plaza and peeled fresh mangos and bananas, which I dipped in peanut butter. We lay on our backs holding hands and watched clouds drift slowly across a sky framed in rustling green leaves. Soft bird songs and gentle breezes stirred the air.

With permission from the caretaker, we waited until the last carload of visitors departed then pitched our tent at one end of the parking lot. Just as we finished blowing up the air mattresses, one of the caretaker's children, a little girl about ten with a long, black ponytail and a bright, embroidered Mayan skirt, approached and shyly asked if we would like to join the family for dinner.

Amongst boisterous laughter and halting Spanish, we scooped fresh pico de gallo onto slivers of roasted chicken nestled in warm, homemade corn tortillas. We added charred green onions, still crisp on the inside, a squeeze of lime, and then sprinkled them with cilantro so freshly cut, it left our fingertips green. We talked about politics, religion, and the meaning of life, treating the language struggles as a stimulating challenge, not a barrier.

After dinner, our host invited us to explore the ruins under the full moon. At the city gate, he stopped to request permission from the gods to enter, using a mixture of Mayan and Christian words, then sprinted from one side of the lower court to the other, whooping and hollering, to demonstrate the mysterious acoustic qualities of the ancient city. A primal current coursed through the darkness, riding the waves of sound.

Despite my shyness when it came to singing in public, and likely because of the dark, I asked if I could sing a song. Unbeknownst to me, while I reveled in the resonance, Tom climbed the twelve stories to the top of the Temple of the Sun.

As the echoes from my melody faded, the voice of the caretaker off to one side of the plaza said, "Hey Tom, are you ready?"

"Yes," Tom said, then he coughed nervously.

Chirping crickets and buzzing insect sounds grew in intensity as I stood there, and then above the cacophony, I heard Tom's voice descend from the blackness. "Candace, under the moon and the stars and the sky above, in the presence of the gods and goddesses and fairies, will you marry me?" His voice, clear and strong, sounded as if he were standing right next to me, but I could not see him. I would discover the next morning that he was over a quarter mile away.

I closed my eyes, basking in the moment, then replied, "Yes."

Suddenly, I could hear his breaths, sharp and quick, and the sounds of footsteps as he descended the temple stairs. It seemed to take forever until he found me in the center of the square. My body tingled with a combination of anticipation and fulfillment, contrasting and compounding each other in a way I'd never experienced before.

We spent Christmas and New Year's Day in Ciudad del Carmen, lounging by an expat's pool after calling our families with news of our engagement. I don't remember how they reacted because I didn't care, but we decided not to wait to tie the knot. We knew we wouldn't want a big fancy wedding, so we chose to go back to Edzna the following week and exchange vows standing atop the Temple of the Moon. We didn't have a legal piece of paper, but we had each other.

CHAPTER 11

January 1997
7 Years Old

As Michael's seventh birthday approached, the recurring unease and lingering sorrow seeped into my awareness, but instead of shunting it away, I confided in Tom. We were staying in a bungalow in Taxco, taking a break from the road for a few days.

Without a pause, Tom asked, "What do you want to do to celebrate?"

"Huh? Celebrate?" I'd always greeted the anniversary of Michael's birth with solitary sadness, setting aside time alone with my drawer of keepsakes. I'd brought none.

"We could go out for a nice dinner. Do you remember that restaurant overlooking the zocalo with the little private decks? Let's go there." He grabbed my hands, and his eyes lit with an inner warmth.

"So, tell me about him," Tom said after we'd ordered, and the waiter had poured wine.

I couldn't remember the last time anyone asked me about Michael.

"Well, he looks like me. A lot actually," I smiled to myself. "But he also looks like his adopted family."

Tom raised his eyebrows.

"Yeah, I know, weird, huh? It's kind of freaky, but all three guys, Michael, John, and David, have the same roundness of face, reddish complexion, and blond hair. It's cool, actually."

"Do you miss him?"

"Yes." Tears formed in my eyes. "And no."

He reached above the table, and I placed my hand in his. He waited.

"How can I miss something I've never had?" I sobbed as quietly as I could.

"I never thought about it like that. I'm sorry." His fingers caressed mine, but he gave no sign of discomfort, surprise, or haste.

I wiped my eyes with the crisp cloth napkin.

"Well," he said, raising his wine glass, "happy birthday to Michael."

"Happy birthday, Michael," I echoed as our glasses clinked.

Tom's ease and openness about Michael were a wonder to me. Grant had never asked about Michael, and although his lack of interest may have been unintentional, I'd internalized it to mean he was ashamed of my past, just like I was, and it was best left in the closet.

There was no update waiting on our return to Minnesota, so I prepared a three-page detailed narrative to send to Jane and David. I included photos from our bike trip and excitedly shared our adventure, sheepishly admitting we'd not made it to the tip of South America but had made it to Alaska. I requested the promised update and eagerly awaited its delivery, but over two months passed before one arrived, and when it did, it was aloof too, like the last one. There were fewer photographs, and the letter felt hurried and inconvenient, referencing that they'd just moved into a new house, that life was hectic and scattered, so the update had fallen through the cracks. They apologized again. I felt like an intruder into their world but tucked the pictures and update into my dresser drawer, still confident Michael was thriving.

Tom took me out to dinner again for Michael's birthday the following year. I'd shared my cherished pictures and updates and cried with quiet reservation on his shoulder on Mother's Day and Christmas, so when no update arrived, he collected me in his arms and patiently waited for the wave of grief to pass. He insisted on accompanying me to the adoption agency, but the visit confirmed what I already knew: I had no choice in the matter. I had signed away any rights long ago. Even though they had agreed to send updates, there was no legal obligation for them to do so, and there was absolutely nothing I could do about it.

I didn't want to believe they wouldn't keep their end of the bargain. But suddenly, it struck me that, despite the promise to send updates, were it not for the formal requests through the agency, I wouldn't have received one the last three years.

My gut turned to stone.

Flailing for a semblance of control, I decided not to request more updates. If I didn't ask for one, I wouldn't feel the crushing disappointment if they didn't send one—that easy. Besides, I told myself, they were busy taking kids to soccer and little league, immersed in piano lessons and family dinners. And if life was moving on for them, maybe I should let it move on for me too? Who was I to cause stress in their lives? Shouldn't they be allowed to live without me looking over their shoulders? I was a distraction and inconvenience they didn't need. So, I wrote to them. I told them they did not need to send any more updates unless they wanted to. Besides, hadn't they proven that they were a model family through the updates so far? That they've provided what I expected?

In my fantasy, they were living the perfect life, and I wasn't a part of it.

I never considered their life might *not* be perfect.

Did I expect a reply? No. But deep down, I hoped for an apology and a reaffirmation of their promise to send letters. And when that did not happen, I flipped the script: lack of contact was *good*. The best thing would be for him never to want contact. It would mean he had everything he needed, which is what I wanted, right?

CHAPTER 12

Six Years Later—May 2003
13 Years Old

Wall-to-wall windows overlooked the small boat harbor from the busy dining room, and beyond the marina, late morning sunshine illuminated the waves rolling up the fjord. The whitecaps flickered like flashbulbs. Every table at The Stow Away Café's annual Mother's Day brunch was filled, its charming mermaid décor and eclectic Thai-fusion menu a favorite among Skagway locals. Tom and I had moved there from Minnesota shortly after our bicycle trip. The snowcapped Alaskan mountains and small-town intimacy were a perfect combination of beautiful scenery and community.

"You're a mother and deserve to be here for Mother's Day too, you know?" Tom said, sipping a mimosa. His blue eyes, which changed hues with the type of lighting, shone like sapphires. He'd left his hair down, at my request, and it curled in tight ringlets around his shoulders.

I wiped my eyes and smiled lamely.

"What's going on in that head of yours?"

"For some reason, this year feels harder. I don't know how to describe it," I said, my shoulders slumped.

"Do you want to go home?"

"No. I *want* to be here." I leaned in. "Here, I can proclaim my motherhood without having to talk to people—I can be anonymous. Does that make sense?"

Patient as always, when it came to Michael, Tom nodded for me to continue.

"I try to tell myself no news is good news, but I wish I knew what was going on in his life. I haven't gotten an update in six years! He's already thirteen!" I shook my head.

"Why don't you talk about him more often?"

"Because it's too hard," my tongue swelled on the last word, and it caught in my throat.

He waited.

"Besides, what would I say? I don't know anything new, and I don't want to rehash the same stuff over and over!" Hot tears rolled down my cheeks. Having no control over the situation crushed my spirit, so I tried to block Michael from my mind most of the time. I hadn't re-read the updates from when Michael was little in more than two years; I'd wrapped them up and placed them in a storage tub.

"Oh, come on. You need to talk about how you feel," he cajoled.

I knew he was right, but…

"All right, fine. I'm sad, and I'm mad, but none of these feelings will change anything." I blew out a frustrated breath. Sudden anger turned inward, and I gulped. "I don't deserve to be unhappy because this was my choice – all of it is *my choice*," I hissed. "*I* gave him away. *I* gave up any rights to him."

Tom shook his head and reached for my hand, but I continued to refuse his advances.

If I'd been counseling someone in my situation, I would have done the same thing as Tom, encouraging them to talk, express their feelings, and *feel* their feelings, but no matter how much time passed, I was unable to show myself any compassion. Tom didn't push me that day or any day, but he never turned his back on me, and he refused to put a time limit on my grief. If only I could learn to do the same.

"Happy Mother's Day," someone said, walking by.

Tearing up for the umpteenth time that day, I fought to regain my composure.

"Happy Mother's Day to you, too," Tom said quickly before they were out of earshot. He reached over the table again, silently requesting my hand. As I felt the warmth of his palm, I let the tears flow.

I allowed myself to think about Michael on his birthday and Mother's Day. It was impossible not to. And Tom developed a habit of asking me how I wanted to honor the occasion two weeks ahead of time, which helped in two ways. First, by referring to these events as positive, I was slowly learning to shift my perspective. Second, I discovered that I could purposefully assess my state of mind by preparing in advance and then decide what to do rather than have the day sneak up on me.

If I were feeling vulnerable, I'd crank up Pink Floyd's "Thin Ice," losing myself in lyrics that always seemed written just for me.

Don't be surprised,

When a crack in the ice

Appears under your feet

You slip out of your depth and out of your mind

With your fear flowing out behind you

As you claw the thin ice.

Or, I'd hike up to Lower Lake and let the chatter of squirrels and creaking trees cover my sounds of sadness. Sometimes, I let myself daydream about him. I'd picture a boyish version of myself at whatever age he happened to be, then sob uncontrollably at the futility of my thoughts.

But, if I were feeling capable, we'd go out to dinner, or Mother's Day brunch, like today.

"Hey, you two!" said Jan, pausing in front of our table. "Are you celebrating Mother's Day?"

I stiffened, even though I knew this would happen. *You can do this.* I nodded.

Her face and eyes bright, she asked, "Do you have children?"

I inhaled slowly. Jan and I were still just getting to know each other, and at Tom's urging, I was trying to be more open about Michael's existence, so I plunged ahead. "Yes, a thirteen-year-old son, Michael."

Jan stood smiling, waiting for more.

I fought the reflex to shut down. "I placed him for adoption when he was a baby."

"Oh, wow, I didn't know that." Her hand touched my arm briefly, and her face remained open and serene.

"It was before Tom and I were together." I searched for something that wasn't too distressing and added, "It was one of the first open adoptions in the state of Minnesota. I was able to choose the parents and even met them."

"That's wonderful! Do you ever get to see him?"

I sat, my back now board-like in its rigidity, my whole body hardening against the truth.

"No, but I received updates and pictures until he was eight." My eyes fell.

What else could I say? That I was unprepared, incapable of being a mom, and had to give him away? That I'm a horrible person? That they quit sending me updates, and I had no recourse?

That I wished he was here?

I trembled, and new tears collected in my eyes, brimming quickly. I lowered my head, and the fat drops fell, splashing as they hit my floral polyester dress. I silently pleaded with her to leave.

"What a beautiful gift you gave them, Candace." Jan's words, delivered with another gentle touch and with such kindness, only served to heighten my distress. "I hope you have a wonderful Mother's Day," she said and walked away.

I bolted up, the chair scraping loudly on the wood floor, and sought refuge in the restroom.

My blood-shot eyes and blotchy red face in the mirror made me cringe, and I watched as a new round of anguish played across my features. Tears pooled then spilled over lips drawn back in a harrowing grimace, which just fed my misery with a reminder that I was an ugly crier.

When the wave of emotion passed, I moistened a paper towel with cold water and held it to my cheeks. "You're okay," I said, trying to soothe myself before going back out to join Tom.

He smiled cautiously. "Are you all right?"

"Yeah. I'm okay."

"Have you called and talked to my mom lately?"

"No. I should, though."

Tom's mom, Dee, was a rare gem: kind, affectionate, and thoughtful. Since the day she learned about Michael, she'd never missed sending me a card on his birthday and Mother's Day, and they always arrived early – no small feat with us living in Alaska. I'd come to refer to her as an angel on Earth, and I was sure this was where Tom had learned his quiet patience and unconditional love.

The lilting sound of Bing Crosby singing "It's Beginning to Look A Lot Like Christmas" drifted amidst multiple conversations, accented by strings of blinking white lights which ringed my friend, Kathy's, vaulted kitchen/dining room. A plump pine tree protruded from the corner, and the silvery strings of icicle tinsel fluttered whenever someone walked by. The decibel level of conversations had steadily increased over the past two hours as the group of a dozen women sipped mulled wine and spiked apple cider.

Kathy's a party planner extraordinaire and a frequent hostess. My favorite gatherings are always the women-only, wintertime parties. Deep conversations morph into boisterous board games or soaks in the outdoor hot tub, where star-filled skies appear sporadically beyond the steam which whips around our heads.

At this holiday social, several women were gearing up to head out for a soak, but I continued my conversation with Gigi, who'd just moved to town a couple of months before. The wine lessened my inhibitions, and without pause, I answered her question regarding kids, "I have a son I placed for adoption at birth."

"Oh my God! I could never do that," she said, then caught herself. "Oh, I'm sorry, I didn't mean…"

The blood drained from my face and cut in automatically, "No, that's all right. I totally get it." Normally her type of response would shut me down, but there was something about Gigi. I liked her. Maybe she could understand. Plus, Tom had been encouraging me to be more open. And, of course, there was the wine. "I was young, and alone, and broke. And I was scared as hell." A stinging sensation began behind my sinuses.

She nodded and sipped her cider.

"I, um, didn't have anything to give him, no way to take care of him, I, um…" I wanted to tell her I wished I could have kept him. I wanted her to know I did the best I could at the time. I didn't want her to think I was a bad person. But the words dammed up as the tears broke free, and I couldn't talk and cry at the same time.

She frowned and stepped back, brushing up against the tree and setting the tinsel a-twinkle. "I'm sorry." Her face seemed to hold sympathy and condemnation. "I didn't mean to make you cry."

"It's okay," I said and turned away. I have no idea why I always tried to ease other people's discomfort, but the last thing I wanted to do was stand there bawling while she felt responsible. I'd planned to collect myself and come back to the conversation, but the self-judgment, buoyed by her initial comment, *Oh my God! I could never do that*, sent me reeling into the bathroom, then calling Tom for a ride home.

When I did share Michael's existence, I discovered people rarely asked about him again. I figured it was because no one in their right mind wants to bring up something that makes the other person cry. I certainly didn't, so I couldn't blame them. Usually, if I saw a conversation heading toward children, I found ways to excuse myself, or while listening to friends brag about their children's achievements, I remained silent, hoping no one would ask. And while there were times when sharing Michael's story felt liberating, I always knew I was opening myself up for others to judge me. And I did a good enough job of that myself. But the more I practiced, the easier it became to say his name aloud without an immediate waterworks show. It was slow, but it was progress.

Once I was asked, "Do you and Tom have kids?"

"No," I said because *we* didn't, but the remorse and self-loathing that accompanied that response ground into my soul like road rash. I'm still picking out bits of gravel. Why did I say it? Maybe the instinct for self-preservation over-powered all else, even reason.

The year Michael turned fourteen, I discovered that my friend, Gloria's, granddaughter, Serena, was one day younger than Michael. Gloria's infectious laughter and down-to-earth approach to life were reason enough to hang around, but soon I found myself more attuned to Serena's movements and whereabouts. I observed her and her classmates at sporting events and other school programs, looking for fashion trends, music choices, and other clues to what Michael might be like, and then fantasized about it.

"How would you feel about getting a dog?" I asked Tom one spring day as we walked out to Yakatania Point. The trail teemed with seasonal residents and their dogs, who had flooded back to town before the start of the summer season. The brisk north wind slapped our faces, carrying the sticky scent of cottonwood buds sprouting along the path.

"I don't know. Seems like a lot of work."

"Awe, come on, it would be fun. Plus, he could go for runs with me in the morning, and it would help us stay active."

"Yeah, I suppose," he shrugged. But he was not enthusiastic in the least.

Over the next few months, I brought it up with increased eagerness, and when Tom reminisced about Rocky, the Pomeranian he'd had growing up, I knew I had him. Once he was on board, we spent almost a full year negotiating what kind of dog we would get. I wanted a dog who could go for runs with me to alert me to bears and other wildlife on the trails. Tom wanted a lap dog like he had as a kid. Tom won. He won because I needed him to *want* a dog too so that we could raise it together.

We didn't want a pure breed or to pay a hefty fee, so I watched rescue websites and regularly checked in with the Juneau and Whitehorse shelters. Then one day at work, an opportunity arrived.

"A little girl came into the gallery today," I blurted to Tom when he walked in after work. "She was bouncing off the walls with excitement for her new puppy, who she'd just met on the drive down from Whitehorse."

It was early September 2005, and bright golden leaves covered the cottonwood trees. The sun's position, already hidden behind Face Mountain at 5:00 pm, was the unmistakable herald of the changing season.

He raised his eyebrows. "And?"

"She showed me a picture, and her mom said they had one puppy left." I stood on the balls of my feet and leaned toward him. "The litter's in Carcross. She gave me the phone number. Can I call?" We had planned to adopt an older rescue dog, not a puppy, so I wasn't sure he'd be open to it.

The corners of his lips lifted, and he nodded. I sprinted for the phone.

The following weekend, Tom cradled a three-pound fuzzball against his chest. She was a mix of Shih Tzu, poodle, and who knew what else, with little beady black eyes and a tiny dot for a nose. She crawled up and nestled atop his shoulder, then disappeared into his long, curly hair. Tom's eyes, filled with wonder and tenderness, met mine, and that was it.

We couldn't agree on a name, so we let her choose when we picked her up. After calling out several names, her head popped up for "Luna." It fit her moon-white fluffiness perfectly. We added Balloona before the end of the first day, the rhyme rolling naturally off our tongues, then Gizmo, because she looked like a Gremlin. In the weeks to follow, we added Gadget—I can't remember why—and Falkor because she looked like a Luck-Dragon when she laid down, head resting between her paws.

Luna Baloona Gizmo Gadget Falkor. My new love.

I did everything the books, experts, and laypersons recommended: I brushed her hair and teeth daily and trained her to sleep in a crate and not beg for food. I used play as a reward instead of treats to teach her commands because we didn't want a fat little dog. Our friend, Jack, a town elder and an artist urged us to make her homemade food, which we supplemented with the best brands of kibble we could get, flown in from the lower-48.

Luna relied on me for everything. And with her addition to our home, I proved that I could take care of a dependent being. I didn't realize it at the time, but that's what I was doing. I hadn't believed I was capable.

In July 2007, Tom and I took days off to attend the Atlin Music Festival, a three-day event in nearby Northern British Columbia featuring a mix of bluegrass, country, and rock-n-roll. With almost ten years of employment with our respective employers, we'd earned the ability to take time off during peak season. We pitched our tent, played music with our tent neighbors for an hour, and then walked into town.

"Well, how about kids?" he asked. It was mid-day, and the lounge connected to the only hotel in town hadn't been inundated with festivalgoers yet, so we grabbed an outdoor table. The timing was perfect for one of our yearly life assessment discussions. We'd already covered jobs, travel, music, and had moved on to the five-year plan.

"No, I don't think so," I said, putting my feet up on an extra chair, leaning back. "I feel like we're good the way we are. We hardly ever fight, and I'm sure that would change if we had a child."

"True." He paused. "Yeah, I'm pretty content with what we have together. I'm not sure I'd want to add another person. I know that may sound selfish, but I like things the way they are."

"I think it's just as selfish to have babies. There are too many people already. Too much poverty, too much pollution."

Tom motioned to the waitress to bring another round of ciders. "Besides, they're expensive. And stinky." He grinned.

I snorted. "We'd have to quit having rehearsals in the living room." Our band, the Hot Toddies, practiced Friday nights at our place. The recent addition of horns to the mix brought the decibel level up several notches, which Luna hated. Lately, she retreated to the back bedroom during practice, as far away from the noise as she could get.

"You know, I've always worried I'd be a bad mom. That's one of the reasons I placed Michael. Now, though, I think I'd mostly be overprotective. Like Georgia, how she never lets Kevin climb trees. Or Danny? Remember when he freaked out about Lucas eating dirt?"

"Yeah, maybe. But," Tom said, serious again, "I think we'd be good parents."

"You'd be such a great dad. Just like Pops," I said, smiling at the thought of Tom's dad. "You are so lucky, you know. Your parents are amazing."

"Sometimes, I think my mom loves you more than me," he chuckled. "She always takes your side."

"She's just trying to keep things even. She's a peacemaker and doesn't want you and Pops to gang up on me." I shooed away a buzzing fly, then took another sip of cider. "You know what? I think your mom is the nicest person I've ever met. She never forgets a birthday or anniversary, always sends thinking-of-you cards, and when we visit, she somehow finds out what our current favorite treats are and stocks the cabinets." I shook my head in appreciation.

"Yay! Milk-duds!" He laughed, then more seriously, "They might be sad if we never have kids. But they'd be sad if we had them and lived so far away too."

"I guess the question is - do we want to?" I asked.

He held my gaze, "I don't, at least for right now."

Every year, as we revisited the issue, we kept coming to the same conclusion for the same reasons. The older we got, the more we made fun of the idea. Whenever we witnessed a public temper tantrum, one of us would turn to the other and say, "Hey, wanna have five of those?"

But, as the years went by, a new realization had surfaced. I don't know exactly when it happened or took full form in my heart. The most significant reason for not wanting to have more children was the need to prevent Michael from feeling as though he wasn't good enough to keep, but another child was.

CHAPTER 13

Five Years Later - January 2008
17 Years Old

Forty-mile-an-hour gale force winds lashed down Skagway's streets, polishing them to glare ice and making footing treacherous. Everything seemed draped in grey: the buildings, the trees, the sky. I slipped off my YakTrax—the spiky grippers used to walk around outside—and held the Post Office door for Mr. Heinz. He smiled warmly; a half dozen packages loaded in his arms.

We hadn't had mail delivery for more than a week due to weather conditions, so when I opened our post office box, a larger than usual stack clogged the opening. It took three tries to free it all from the narrow confines. I quickly leafed through, tossing junk mail in the big trash can, but then stopped abruptly at a five-by-seven manila envelope. The return label included the first name and last initial from an unfamiliar Minnesota address.

My heart skipped a beat.

It was an update. It had to be. It couldn't be a coincidence. Michael would turn eighteen in two days, and all previous updates from the agency had looked similar.

My hands shook as I struggled to replace the grippers over my shoes, and although I walked the three blocks home, it felt as though I sprinted—excitement and apprehension pulsed through my veins.

I threw the other mail on the table, went straight to the bedroom, and switched on the light. The dark paneling seemed to devour the illumination, so I clicked on the nightstand lights too. Sitting at the edge of our bed, I cradled the envelope as if it were a porcelain doll. It was at least half an inch thick. *There must be photos inside.* A tingling sensation crept up my spine.

Scotch tape covered the two-pronged metal clasp, so I carefully broke the seal, folded back the flap, and peeked inside—a stack of pictures nestled beside several sheets of paper. My hands shook as I tipped the envelope up, and the pile of prints slipped into my palm. Then, I pulled out and unfolded the paper to reveal a messily written letter on lined notebook paper, the jagged edges unevenly trimmed off.

Resolutely I set aside the photos, closed my eyes, and held my breath for a moment. I had been waiting ten years for this, hoping against hope that he would want to reach out to me. My heartbeat pulsed in my temples and neck. I exhaled slowly and opened my eyes. Familiar handwriting began:

12/31/07
Candace,
We hope everything is going well for you and your family. I know it has been a very long time since you have heard from us, and I apologize for that as I am sure that you have spent time wondering and worrying about how Michael was doing.

I sighed and furrowed my brow. *Well, that's an understatement.*

Jane was always good about letters and pictures for you. About eight years ago, Jane passed away of a suicide.

What? What!
I lowered the letter. My first thought was not for Jane but Michael. *How could she? How could she leave him? She was supposed to take care of him. Oh my God, she abandoned him!*

She was a wonderful woman, and we miss her greatly. Michael was ten, and John was fourteen. At the time, we had just returned home from a trip to New York City and Washington D.C. It was very difficult for all of us as it was so unexpected.

What had I done? How could I have chosen so poorly!

By sheer force of will, I continued reading:

Someday we will have the chance to explain more. It was a hereditary thing that was part of Jane's family.

Since I had family and friends who had experienced depression, I knew what depression looked like and what havoc it could wreak. But I'd never experienced suicide first-hand. I wanted to crumple the pages and hurl the letter from me, but I couldn't. Pulling myself back from the betrayal, I kept going.

We had moved back to our hometown before this happened as there was an opportunity for me, and I had been traveling a lot. It was a blessing because we had a tremendous amount of support from friends and relatives. Michael, John, and I adjusted to our new life without Jane. It has all turned out ok; as you well know, life takes on different directions for many different reasons.

When Michael was fourteen, I remarried, and we moved to a larger community that was just down the road from us. My wife, Lori, is an RN responsible for the emergency room. She has four daughters. Now ages nineteen to twenty-nine. We also have three granddaughters, of which two live with us most of the time.

Michael has a girlfriend, Hannah, and he and Hannah spend a lot of time with the little girls (Haley, eight, and Mikayla, four). She is a sophomore in high school, a cute girl—she has made Michael happy.

I tried to picture him old enough to have a girlfriend, but he was still just a little boy in my mind.

He has struggled with school, and we hope we can get him through graduation. He is a very bright young man but isn't good at getting his homework done. He took his ACT and got a 23 but will take it again as he forgot his calculator. ORGANIZATION is what Michael struggles with the most. When it comes to chemistry and math, he is at the top of the class.

So he's like me and not like me. I never completed homework on time as a kid, but I sucked at math and science.

Michael has always been a good loving kid. He has had many opportunities to enjoy traveling and different areas of the country.
We live in southwest Minnesota and have enjoyed the opportunity to enlarge our family with new siblings and nieces and nephews around. Our house has always been pretty active, with lots of people coming and going.

I took a much-needed deep breath, feeling my shoulders relax just a bit. *Big, extended family. Good.*

I hope this has not been too much rambling for you. There is just so much to tell you and share.

Yes, yes! I know.

We hope that you are doing well. Michael and I have talked about what it would be like to have the two of you meet.

Again, I felt my heart beating in my throat and could now hear the double whoosh in my ears.

I know that will be important to him when the time is right.

Please, oh please.

John, in contrast, has never really shown an interest in meeting his biological family. Not sure why. John is still at our house pretty much every day and is a really good person. Both Michael and John are good people. That makes me very proud when people tell me that they visited one of them, and our friends tell us what good kids they are. They both have their days, but I know how blessed I have been to have had the opportunity to share my life with them.
Thank you for the gift you have given us. Again, I hope this finds you doing well.
With Love,

David, Lori, Michael, John, and the rest of the bunch

Then, a postscript; written in blue ink. The first part had been in black ink. I had no way of knowing when he'd added it in comparison to the first part.

In talking to Michael, I can tell he looks forward to meeting you and building a relationship. He is a <u>lucky boy</u>.
Dave

Tears streamed down my cheeks. I rushed to brush them aside, collecting them on my shirt sleeve. I didn't want them to damage the letter. Finally, though, tears of joy after all these years.

There was one more piece of paper. I guessed David had added it as an afterthought, and probably with trepidation. It was brave.

Cream-colored personalized stationery. It contained only a few words.

Candace,
My cell phone if you would like to contact us.
Dave

He'd included his last name, followed by his phone number.

Then, toward the bottom, just above a two-inch black and white illustration of a sprawling residence, two words with an arrow pointing down to the sketch:

Michael's House

I set the letter aside and went to the bathroom to wipe my eyes and blow my nose. Returning to the edge of the bed, I grabbed the photos and sifted through them slowly. Almost four dozen four-by-six prints, some with writing on the back, in random order.

A laughing Michael, at ten years of age, captured in mid-squirm as an aunt kissed his cheek. I held the photo against my breast as I picked up another.

Michael, John, and David posing at a scenic overlook. 2006. *His face is exactly the same shape as mine!*

Stepsister Janelle with daughter Page, petting a horse.

Multiple pictures of Lori, David's new wife, and her daughters and granddaughters, lots of platinum-blond hair, and big blue eyes, all posing dramatically for the camera.

Six snapshots of Michael and John, ages unknown, yet easy to follow the progression of years. Chubby boys with double chins morphed into cool teenagers sporting dyed black hair, throwing peace signs.

Michael in the bathtub, probably around seven years old, bubbles piled high on his head and under his chin. *Adorable.* Another of him hanging by both hands from a tree branch.

Then, a photo of Jane reading to Michael and another of her with both boys at Disney World. Bile rose in my throat. *No! Stop it!*

And pictures of Michael with Hannah, their eccentricities expressed by her electric blue hair and his gauged ears and nose ring. I drank in the sight, reveling in their individuality and delightful weirdness. Then, turning it over, I found another treasure written on the back.

Hannah and Loverboy
Michael is very good to Hannah
He treats her with a tremendous amount of respect

My heart sang.

I lingered over the photos and reread the letter multiple times; then, I called Tom.

He found me on the bed, now cross-legged, with the photos spread out around me in a semi-circle, grouped by age as best I could, and spaced perfectly between the blocks of Tom's blue-ribbon mariner's compass quilt.

"Look." I picked up the letter, unfolded my legs, and stood, holding it out to him. He reached for me instead, taking me into his arms. I cried until his shirt was soaked with snot and tears. Finally, I let go. "Read it," I said as I went to grab a roll of toilet tissue.

Tom's weight settled on the other side of the bed, and he read while I continued to look at the photos, picking up one at a time, soaking in the images like rainwater in a desert.

When he got to the piece of stationery, he looked up, "Do you want to call him?"

I'm sure he already knew the answer, but I replied, "Yes."

"Okay. Do it." He glanced at the clock on the nightstand. "It's eight o'clock there, not too late to call." His eyes sparkled with excitement.

I grabbed the portable phone and threw caution to the wind.

"Hello?"

"Hi. David?"

"Yes?"

"This is Candace."

"Oh Candace," a long, heavy sigh, "I'm so happy you called."

As he said my name, my chest bloomed with warmth.

His voice took on a husky quality, and he choked, "So happy."

Cross-legged once again, I hunched over, folding in on myself. "I just got your letter today. I can't even express how thankful I am." My throat was already swollen and sore. "I never thought it would come. But," the following words came out as a croak, "but I always hoped." I labored to collect myself, not wanting to sob in his ear. Finally, I asked, "How is he?"

"He's good. He looks like you."

"Yeah, I saw the photos." I smiled, touching the one of him in the bathtub. "Thank you for these."

"Candace, I'm so sorry I haven't been in touch."

It doesn't matter. All that matters is that he's okay. He is okay, isn't he?

"I don't know what else to say. I'm sorry, though."

I winced. I couldn't respond to this. And I couldn't ask: *How could she? What happened?* I did not want to do or say anything to jeopardize this tenuous link. "So, where are you in Minnesota?"

"We're in Marshall. Down by Sioux Falls. Do you know where that is?"

"Yes. It's nice to know where Michael is now. I don't know why really, but it is."

"Where are you?"

"We're in Alaska and have been now for almost ten years. I mentioned we'd worked for a summer in Skagway the last time I wrote, right? Well, we moved here the following year." Almost jumping over my own words, I added, "But most of my family are still in Minnesota. We drive down every year to visit."

I'm there every year. Just say the word.

"I'm the director of an art gallery, and Tom is the Chief Maintenance Engineer for a large local hotel."

Is it too soon to ask? Michael, where's Michael? I don't want to be rude, but…

"We've always wanted to take a cruise to Alaska!" His voice was light and cheerful. "How wonderful it must be!"

"That's how most people get here. We get almost a million visitors off cruise ships every year." My guard slipped as I fell into my habit of sharing about where I lived. People commonly asked about life in Alaska, a safe and easy place for the conversation to move.

David worked at Archer Daniels Midland, a name I recognized. *That's right.* I closed my eyes, nodding to myself—*a good, well-paying job.*

I told him how long Tom and I'd been together.

Now? Is it still too soon? Yeah, too soon. Come on!

Finally, though, I couldn't wait any longer. I had to know and slipped to the edge of the bed, toes touching the floor. "Is Michael there? Do you think he'd want to talk to me?"

"He's downstairs. Just give me a second. I'll go check."

I stopped breathing.

CHAPTER 14

January 2008
2 Days Until 18th Birthday

"I'm gonna talk to Michael," I silently mouthed as I pointed at the phone.

Tom was leaning casually against the kitchen counter.

"I think," I shrugged and raised my eyebrows, holding one hand palm up in the universal sign of uncertainty.

When he looked up, wide-eyed, I realized he'd been straining to listen in. I'd instinctively concealed myself in the bedroom—my modus operandi—but I couldn't contain my excitement.

He pushed away from the counter to stand inches from me. We locked gazes. I chewed the inside of my lower lip.

Muffled voices, then, "Candace?" David again, his voice clear as he came back on the line.

My eyes grew big. "Yeah?"

"Here's Michael."

My feet seemed to lift off the ground, and colors swirled around me, aura-like, as I finally let out the breath I didn't realize I'd held. The jostling as the receiver changed hands echoed in my ears.

"Hi, Mike here." His voice high-pitched and breathy, boyish yet confident.

I floundered and twirled in place, not sure if I should sit down, walk around, or fly to the moon.

I stilled. "Hi, Mike," I exhaled his name. It felt strange to say it. I'd always referred to him as Michael. The shortened version felt odd and almost stuck to my tongue. "I can't believe it's you. I'm so glad to hear your voice."

"Wow, this is weird, huh?" No anxiety or uncertainty, just casual acceptance. *Is this just a teenager thing – acting cool? Is he not as freaked out as I am?*

"Yeah, I know. How are you? Are you doing okay?" I walked to the bedroom and sank onto the bed.

"Yeah, I'm good. Dave's taken good care of me."

"Dave? Your dad? You call him by his first name?" My back snapped straight as alarm bells clanged in the back of my mind. *Does he have a contentious relationship with David?*

"Yeah, I call him Dave to other people. I have since I was a kid." His tone made it sound reasonable and completely unremarkable. "Like, since I was twelve or so."

I almost laughed at him, thinking eighteen was much older, but successfully suppressed it.

"I call him Dad too, but mostly at home when it's just the family."

The ringing bells receded, and my posture softened.

I wanted to ask if he was happy, but I wasn't sure if I was ready for the answer. I knew I would likely be jealous and bitter if he were and self-flagellate if he weren't. *But where to begin?*

I wanted to know everything that very second, but I also wanted to savor each tiny detail. Indecision paralyzed me.

"Where was I born?" he asked casually.

"St. Cloud. At the hospital there."

"Oh. I've always kinda wondered."

"You know, you could have asked your dad. He would have told you."

"Yeah, I guess," he said, his voice flat. "I just never thought to."

Did that mean he never thought about me? Suddenly, the self-absorbed teenager I used to be reared her ugly head, and a new round of tears threatened as pressure built in my sinuses.

A pause settled like fog. We were both lost in it, the time and distance between us so vast.

"I don't know what to say," Michael admitted.

"Me neither." I flopped back, lying on the bed. "We're in uncharted territory."

"Could we use the Internet?" he asked. "I mean, like email? To ask questions and stuff?"

"Yes." I bolted upright. "I think that's a great idea."

"Are you on MySpace?"

"Um, no. I'm not sure what that is."

"You should check it out." The energy returned to his voice. "It's a cool website just to hang out on."

"Okay," I said, doubtful. I couldn't say no, though. I didn't want to say "no" to anything my son requested.

I grabbed the piece of stationery with their house on it and wrote down Michael's email address. After exchanging information, though, the fog rolled back in.

"Uhm, I'm gonna go, okay?"

"Okay," I said, relieved yet disappointed.

"Do you want to talk to Dave again?"

"Yes, please. And, thank you, Michael. I really look forward to hearing from you." A heaviness hit me in the chest as the receiver changed hands. I didn't want to let him go but didn't know how to hang on either, just like eighteen years earlier.

"Hey, Candace, seems that went well," David said. He must have stayed close during our conversation. I was glad for his protectiveness. "I know it was short, but I'm guessing this will take a little time. Here, let me give you my email too."

"Thank you, David," I choked. I didn't know how to express how grateful I was, for sending me the update, for including his phone number, for eighteen years of taking care of Michael—all of it—so I just let the words fade away.

"All right," David said. "Let's just see how things play out. I'm here if you want to talk, but I'm hoping you two will take this opportunity to connect. I'm glad you called, and I know Michael is too. Take care."

As the call ended, my body deflated, and I slumped back onto the bed. The conversation went so fast that I could barely keep up, yet it seemed as if it went on forever. *Oh my God! I just talked to Michael!* Suddenly, my exhaustion evaporated, and a new sensation took hold, suffusing my body like the rays of the sun after a passing cloud.

He was okay; he was safe and cared for. And nothing in his tone of voice or mannerisms indicated he was upset or angry. The tension left my shoulders as I released years of pent-up fear.

94

Tom poked his head into the bedroom, bright-eyed. "So, what did he say?"

I shrugged. "Well, neither of us knew what to say. He wants to email back and forth, so I gave him our email address and left it in his court."

"That's a great idea. Let him take the lead." Tom reached for my hands, pulled me to my feet, and folded me in his arms.

I felt raw and exposed, vulnerable in a way I'd never experienced before. Michael *wanted* to communicate with me. And he hadn't accused me of abandonment, as I'd expected. The realization hit like a flash flood, and my knees almost buckled.

"You okay?"

"Yes. I am."

I am.

A sly grin spread across his face, and he headed into the kitchen. "I'd say it's time to celebrate, wouldn't you?"

I nodded. "Michael...," whimsy in my voice. Absentmindedly I leaned up against the counter, then boosted myself up. "Oh my God, Tom, I can't believe it."

"Here's to a future with Michael." He handed me a glass of cabernet. "Wow, it's finally happening. We finally get to know what's going on."

"Yeah, he's on something called MySpace. He said we should check him out on there."

"Well, what are we waiting for?" His smile warmed my heart—and the love in his eyes. And his anticipation fed my eagerness.

"Yes!" I slipped off the counter, lit a cedar-scented candle, then sidled up next to him in front of the desktop screen. "Finally." I leaned back in the chair, waiting for the computer to power up. *Come on.* Squirming, I sipped my wine, set it down, and picked it right back up again. With the stem in both hands, I spun it with my fingertips, the contents swirling up the sides.

After the connecting modem squelched for an eternity, the computerized voice proclaimed, "You've got mail!"

My heart soared—there, at the top of the list, was an email from Michael!

Tom, in control of the mouse and keyboard, immediately clicked on the message. I slid to the front of the chair, angled my feet up onto my tiptoes, and strained forward, willing the message to load faster.

It was short, just one sentence.

I really have no idea where to begin; this is just kinda strange just cause I've always wondered, you know, but what questions do you have for me...
Jurred

Jurred? What did that mean? Did he intend to write Jarred?

Tom searched for MySpace, then for Michael's page. "What are you gonna ask him?"

"I don't know. There's so much I want to know!" Maybe it was the wine—maybe Michael's message—but I was positively giddy.

"Okay, hold on. How about you break it down to just a couple of things to start. You know, try to keep it manageable? I don't think you should overwhelm him. It might scare him off."

"You're right." My thoughts whirled. *How do I even do this?* "Could I start with his favorite foods and things to do?"

"Yeah, exactly."

On MySpace, we discovered he used "Jurred" as his username, and his page was public. Michael's photos were mostly of partying, and I was surprised he wasn't worried about me, or other adults, seeing them. One picture had three people in it, one of whom I thought was him, but their faces were all obscured due to billowing smoke. Another photo showed him amidst a larger group huddled around a small table cluttered with beer cans, plastic cups, and an overflowing ashtray. If he was trying to shock me, it didn't work. I wanted him to be a typical teenager, and I didn't think drinking or smoking was any reason to become alarmed.

Michael's posts were almost exclusively about his girlfriend, Hannah. Every feasible way a teenage boy can say how much he loves his girlfriend, followed by hearts—lots and lots of hearts. We tried to link to Hannah's page, but it was private.

We agreed to create a shared MySpace account. Our hope was to "friend" Michael on the site. Then all our personal information would be available to him anytime. We laughed as we negotiated our choices: favorite movies, books, heroes. We spent the entire evening navigating the site and creating our online profile, finishing two bottles of wine.

The next morning, I sat down to write a reply to Michael. What do you ask your eighteen-year-old child you are just getting to know? Are there off-limits topics? Or things I *should* ask?

I composed the first draft then consulted Tom, which heralded a new level of intimacy with him. We argued the pros and cons and evaluated every single bit of the email, trying to think about how Michael might react. Even how to sign the letter took consideration. Do I use "love" or some other endearment?

In the end, this is what we came up with:

Hi Mike,

So, yes, where to begin.

I have so many questions and want to share so much, but it is hard to figure out where to start. So, I think, maybe take it slow if you're okay with that.

I want to know you're safe, healthy, happy......the list goes on and on......but let's start a little smaller. I'll send a couple of questions with my answers, and you send back your answers and a new question or two. Will this work for you? I hope so....so, here goes:

What is your favorite thing to do right now, and what's your favorite food? My favorite thing to do right now is to play and sing music. My favorite food is.....chocolate, but I like almost everything, and I cook a lot. I recently found out I am allergic to wheat and learned how to cook all over again. (Have you had any problems with food? If so, this wheat allergy runs in the family, so you may want to check it out.)

I have attached four photos—one of where I live near Skagway, Alaska. The photo was taken about 25 miles from my house. One is an older photo (2003) of Tom and me (I will work on getting a more recent one scanned into the computer). One is of us and some friends at Disneyland last spring, and the last is of Luna and me at our Haunted House this past Halloween.

All right, that's it for now. I want to allow you to decide how we proceed here, so if you don't like the question/answer thing, let me know what your ideas are about how we can learn about each other - if that is what you want to do. You tell me what you are hoping will happen with our relationship. A little contact? Lots of contact? And you don't need to decide right this second either.

That's why I think we should take it slow. Anyway, I am rambling here. I'm going to stop now.
   Love,
   Candace

Now we just needed to wait for a response.

CHAPTER 15

The Next Day—January 2008
1 Day Until 18th Birthday

I tried to read. Played guitar. Channel surfed. Filed my nails. Rummaged in the cupboard. Grabbed a handful of cashews, plopped one in my mouth, then threw them away. Back in the recliner, Luna jumped up and settled on my lap, so I picked up the book again but couldn't concentrate, so switched to the remote, clicking mindlessly.

"Stop it, Luna," I snapped. "You've been poking your cold, wet nose against my forearm for the past twenty minutes." Her big brown eyes continued pleading. "Okay, fine, let's go for a walk." She leaped from the couch and headed for the door.

After a quick, frigid walk around the neighborhood, I resumed checking my email practically every fifteen minutes. In between, I attempted to solder links for a silver bracelet, usually an easy task, but they kept melting. After a half dozen attempts, I finally gave up. All my old tricks of avoidance and diversion were not working, perhaps because I'd always used them to block traumatic thoughts and events, and this didn't qualify.

Eleven hours later, Michael responded.

I sighed with relief. This email was longer than his first.

Candace,
Well, first of all, I feel rather off just because I [don't] know who Tom is. Is he my father or someone else? Lol.

Holy crap! Does he think Tom's his father? I must take care of that quickly.

My favorite thing to do would be to be with my g/f, but computers are what I love. Food-wise, I really like most everything. I also like to cook, and I guess I could say I'm rather good at it.

I bobbed my head, smiling. *So confident.*

I am allergic to coconut. Dang, I really hope I'm not allergic to wheat; I can't get enough of it.

Yep, big bummer. I didn't think anyone in my family had a coconut allergy, but maybe it came from Eddie's side. *I should tell him about grandma's cancer, though.*

Hmm... What do you do for a living? Dave said something about like silver or something, but I don't really know. I really love writing, and I was told that you did too. Is this true? And if so, what do you write? I was also told that you traveled a lot, tell of your journeys and stuff.

Yes—tell him about my work and travels—that would be a great way to let him get to know me.

I'm glad that we can do this by email just because, even though I don't have a job or anything, I'm still rather busy with life. Also, it's a lot easier to send photos and whatnot. I've attached a few, mostly of Hannah and I.
-Mike

I downloaded the photographs, opening them full screen. I touched the image of the cowlick in his hair – it was just like mine. After a thorough examination of his pictures, I drafted a response. Over the following couple of hours, I tried to cover all his questions. Satisfied, I showed it to Tom.

"Whoa, whoa, whoa, first off, it's too long."

I huffed and glared at him. He hadn't even read it yet.

"All right, give me a few minutes." He slid up to the desk.

Luna's eyes tracked my movements, her head resting on her paws, as I paced from the living room to the kitchen and back again.

"I don't think you should go into so much detail about Eddie," he said as I stopped to peek over his shoulder. "If he wants to know more, let him ask David."

"Why?"

"It's not your place or responsibility. Besides, you have no idea where he is anyway. And didn't you say his file wasn't 'open'?"

I nodded. "Okay."

"And the info about me seeing you when you were pregnant with him—cut that too."

"Why?"

"It's too much, too soon. Look at this kind of like a first date." Tom spoke as if this should be common sense, but it irked me.

"Oh," I sagged. I would look back in later years and understand that this was sage counsel.

"But I like the travel info. Good stuff. A little wordy, though. Can you tighten it up a bit?"

My head bobbed again. He suggested a few more minor changes, then stood up.

"I'll do some editing, but what do you think otherwise? Am I coming off as an obsessive-compulsive psycho mamma or too needy?"

"No, I think the tone's good. You should sleep on it before sending it, though."

The following morning, after a final read-through, I sent it. I was glad I'd waited; I felt more assured of my answers and confident I didn't come off like an emotional wacko.

Jan 19, 2008
Hi Mike—

Happy 18th! I was going to call you, but I think we are both more comfortable with using email. It is hard for me to believe it has been 18 years since you were born! And, No, Tom is not your birth father! I thought you had information about that from David. Ask him about this, as I think he's the one who can give you direction.

I am a self-employed silversmith and jewelry maker during the winter months, and I sell fine art and jewelry, including my own, during the summer season at a very nice gallery in town. Although I have always enjoyed writing, I have not done much except journaling recently. Tom is encouraging me to write a cookbook for people with wheat allergies, and I have written a bit, but nothing worth showing anyone yet. I'd always thought it would be great to write a sci-fi or fantasy novel, but I don't think I have any storylines. How about you - what do you like to write, and is there anything you'd be interested in sharing?

I did some educational traveling during college, but the best I have done has been with Tom, specifically our bicycle trip. We started in St. Cloud and followed the Mississippi River to West Memphis, across Texas, and down into Mexico. Once in Mexico, we followed the Gulf Coast around to Campeche`. At a ruin called Edzna, we were engaged and returned a week later to say our vows. This is a wonderful story. Someday I'll tell you the detailed version if you'd like. Another great trip was to Glacier Bay National Park, where we traveled by kayak for five days alone in the wilderness. Fantastic - everyone should get the opportunity to do something like that in their lives.

This letter became much longer than I anticipated. I will write again with a couple more questions later. I hope you have a great Birthday.
Candace

Again, I waited.

By the next day, I second-guessed everything. Did I write too much? Is he mad about Tom not being his father? Did I offend him? Has he decided he doesn't want to have a relationship with me?

Finally, after two days, I couldn't stand it. I wrote another letter, hoping to prod him into action.

Hi Mike,
So, here are a couple more questions. Are you into any outdoor or sports activities? Do you like to read and if so, what kinds of books?

I emailed David, too, because I was going out of my mind. I did not send a copy of my exchange with Michael but summarized everything and asked if Michael was okay.

David wrote back early the following day.

Candace,
It sounds like you and Michael have had some good dialogue.
I asked him about how things were going, and he said, "Good!"

The tension that had been living in my shoulders eased.

He said you had shared some medical information with him.
I am sure this will be enlightening for all of us. I believe Michael
will embrace this opportunity to learn about you and Tom and to
share what he is all about with you. He is inquisitive, sensitive, and
thinks of himself as an intellectual. He likes to read books that are
a bit more in-depth than what I would read. I guess he is just trying
to find out what is important in life.
I would follow Tom's advice on the email approach. Michael is
a sensitive and caring kid. He may communicate more regarding
his feelings to you than he would to me. I think that you will have
a great effect on Michael from the standpoint of a woman's sensi-
tivity and way of looking at things. I think he is searching for that.

My heart swelled.

I sometimes take the hardline on things and often wonder how
my approach would be with the boys if Jane were there to offer her
twist on things.

My stomach lurched. Her death was so sad, but my gut reaction
was still anger at the perceived betrayal. *Let it go.* I consciously un-
furrowed my brows.

I know this has been overwhelming for you, as it has been emotional for me as well. Knowing the happiness and fulfillment that this
could bring to both of you is a special gift.
God bless and much love,
Dave and Lori

I wrote back immediately.

Hi Dave,

Thank you for the input. I have always felt good about my decision to place Mike with you and having the opportunity to speak to you again has reaffirmed my choice. I am going to sit back and let this process run its course.

I waited eighteen years; I could hold on a little longer. He was okay. David had proven kind and thoughtful during our interactions, and I had confidence he had Michael's best interest at heart. However slow or little the contact may be, it would have to be enough.

Checking MySpace became a daily routine, watching and waiting. It may not have been a lot, viewing from afar, but it was so much more than what I'd ever had.

Four days later, Michael finally emailed.

Hey hey,

Sorry i haven't written, i have been busy with school, we just started a new semester. I love writing, if i can find my book, i'll send it to you, but i should tell you it's almost 850 pages long,

Eight-hundred-fifty pages! Oh my.

I've been told that it's rather good,

Again, his boyish confidence made me smile.

i don't do much sports and stuff, not really my kinda thing, i would rather sit down at the computer and play an MMORPG or do a little VRML programming.

I opened another browser window and Googled MMORPG and VRML: massively multiplayer online role-playing game and virtual reality modeling languages. *Computer stuff.*

As for reading, yea i read a lot, most sci-fi stuff, but i really love reading books on Hyperspace and Quantum Physics or Time Travel.
Sorry it's so short, I'll try to write more tomorrow,

Oh, I hope so.

W/Love
Mike

He wrote *love*!
"Tom," I yelled, "come look."
"Wow, he wrote 'love.' That's a big deal, I think."
I jumped out of the office chair to make space for Tom, then ran to grab another from the dining room and placed it right next to him, eager for him to read.
"I think it's important that you are careful about how you approach him. I was a teenage boy once, too, you know." Seeing me scowl, his expression softened. "I don't want you to get hurt."
"I know, I know. And I think you're right, I do. I don't want to scare him away, but I just want to know everything right now! And these time lags are killing me!"
"Really? Come on." He shook his head. "You've got to chill out. Give him some time." He stood from the computer, pulling the chair back for me. Once I sat and faced the screen, he put his hands on my shoulders and bent down to kiss the top of my head. "I love you."
"I love you too. Thanks. It's pretty overwhelming."
We agreed that Tom should be as much a part of this budding relationship as possible. I hoped Michael would become an important part of our lives. Therefore, the following day, we replied together.

Hi Mike,
How exciting...a book. I'd love to read it. Since you're interested in time travel, hyperspace, and futuristic topics, have you read the Intervention series by Julian May, that's one of Tom's favorites.
Could you tell me more about MMORPG and VRML programming? I am not that familiar with them.
I didn't know you started a new semester. Any fun classes?
Love,
Candace

Then another prod, three days later.

Hi Mike,
I forgot to send you my address so you can send me your book.

The prospect of reading his book gave me goosebumps.

No hurry.

Actually, I was chomping at the bit.

I look forward to hearing from you again.

I wanted to come across as carefree and laid back. I was anything but.

Love,
Candace

Hours turned into days. Days turned into weeks. Weeks turned into months.
No response.

CHAPTER 16

Four Months Later—May 2008
18 Years Old

The whirring of the bean grinder preceded the aroma of freshly ground coffee, and I inhaled deeply, welcoming its soothing effect. Early morning sunlight filtered through the cottonwood tree into the kitchen, warming my shoulders.

"It's been over three months," I blurted to Tom, who sat in the other room. "Do you think I should email him?" I tried to sound like I'd just thought this and hadn't brooded over it for weeks.

He swiveled the office chair to face me and sighed. "Yeah, okay." He crossed his arms over his chest. "I still think you need to tread lightly. You don't want to scare him away."

"Well, at this point, he's not *here* to scare away. I figure it can't hurt."

"Just make sure you watch your tone." He turned back to the computer screen. "You don't want to come off as pushy."

"Yeah, yeah." I glared at the back of his head and flipped him the finger, then returned to making coffee.

"And don't ask for anything."

"What?" I stomped to the threshold.

He spun back around to look at me. "Don't ask him to write back. Or send you pictures. Nothing."

I shifted all my weight onto one leg and put a hand dramatically on my cocked hip. Stoney faced, I waited. *I'd given him space. Hadn't I been patient?*

He slumped. "I just don't want you to be disappointed if he doesn't respond. That's all." The tenderness in his voice and eyes disarmed me, and I slumped too.

He was right, as usual.

God, I hated that.

My impatience masked anger - at myself. I was the one who'd abandoned Michael. But by focusing on Michael's lack of response, I could deflect the self-loathing that accompanied the acknowledgment of that desertion.

After the most recent email to Michael in January, I'd resolved to let him be in control. The only way I knew how to do it was to revert to my old coping strategy of trying not to think about him at all. And the best way to do that was to keep busy.

And I'd succeeded. For a while anyway.

I'd upped my workout routine, added weight training to my regular winter treadmill program, and then signed up for a marathon. Developing a personalized marathon training program took a solid two days. I'd hung the homemade, four-month, color-coded poster board by the back door where I could enter data daily and track progress.

As vice-president of the Skagway Emblem Club, I'd coordinated volunteers to help with burger feeds, reading initiatives at the library, and high school scholarship programs. In February, the local Cancer Awareness Fund board of directors elected me president. Preparing for their biggest fundraiser, the annual walk-a-thon scheduled for June, was a perfect diversion.

Between volunteer activities and marathon training, I threw myself into my workshop. My small home-based business had made enough money the previous year to expand into new materials and upgrade tools. Tom built me a custom workbench, and I'd added an oxygen/propane torch, a rolling mill, and chasing hammers. I lost myself for hours in the practice of soldering with pinpoint accuracy and began numerous new projects with the ability to roll out my own sterling silver sheet and wire.

Michael's postings on MySpace had diminished, so I quit checking it as frequently to reduce my disappointment. Again, I told myself that he would reach out if he needed me. I desperately wanted to believe that if he didn't, it meant he was doing okay. And if he were okay, then I could ease up on my self-flagellation.

The approach of Mother's Day, the first since our reunion, likely played a role in my anxiety, but I did not recognize it at the time. I didn't fully comprehend the impact of special occasions and holidays until later.

After Tom left for work, I drafted the email, attempting to quash the harpy voice in my head that wanted to know why Michael hadn't written. Instead, I tapped into the mother figure I wanted to present to Michael. Tom reviewed it later, and we agreed to send it the following morning.

> *Hi Mike,*
>
> *I just wanted to drop a note and let you know I have been thinking of you. I know graduation is coming up, and I wanted to wish you good luck.*
>
> *Life is busy here as we prepare for the upcoming tourist season. We all put in extra hours this time of year, which is especially hard as the weather is getting to be so nice, and I just want to be outside.*
>
> *I hope everything is going all right with you. Take care.*
>
> *Love,*
>
> *Candace*

A nice, light, hopefully, non-threatening letter.

But I didn't feel any better. Tension throbbed in the back of my skull, my tongue seemed layered in velvet, and I couldn't swallow. A pressure cooker ready to explode, I surged to my feet and strode into the kitchen, yanked open the refrigerator door, then stared, unseeing, until I realized there were no answers in there.

Back at the computer, I checked Michael's MySpace page. Nothing new.

"Come on!" I spun the chair around and sagged, hanging my arms at my sides. Pacing the house again, I disturbed Luna, who'd been sleeping on her pillow, so I grabbed her leash.

The fresh air and bright daylight cleared my head and warmed my face, effectively stopping the cycle of corrupted thoughts. I didn't want to push the uncomfortable feelings away entirely; they were my connection to Michael, but what could I do?

An hour later, back home in front of the computer, I typed "adoption" in a Google search bar. This returned over one million results in less than a minute, most geared toward people seeking to adopt. A quick switch to "birth mother" revealed more relevant results.

This simple act gave me a physical outlet for my pent-up energy and anxiety. Hours slipped away as I relived my placement journey through the eyes of other mothers, crying alongside them through their ordeals. I seethed at broken promises to provide updates and railed against lies told by adoption agencies and family members to coerce women into relinquishing their parental rights. In the end, I latched onto stories of reunion and redemption. My heart thundered to read about how other first moms yearned for yet feared contact and how their feelings and experiences mirrored my own.

I wasn't alone.

"Here," Tom set a glass of water next to me on the desk. "Have you been sitting here all day?"

"Um-hum." More than a dozen tabs lined the top of the screen. My back ached, I had cottonmouth, and a dull throb behind my eyes had evolved into a pinpoint stabbing sensation in my temple.

"You need to take a break. Get up, move around." He grabbed my hands and helped me up. "Find any good info?"

"Definitely. Some great essays and blogs by other birth moms. And you're right; I need a break. Let's make dinner, then watch a movie."

The next day, I woke excited to continue my research. I stopped obsessing about when or if Michael would write back. Instead, I read more reunion stories, hoping to find guidance for my situation.

Initially, I concentrated on adoptee blogs, hoping to discover insight into how Michael might be reacting to our reunion. The stories told of joys and sorrows in reunion, botched get-togethers, and miscommunication as the parties fumbled about trying to build a relationship on a foundation of lost time. Some adoptees *never* wanted to reunite, the anger and sadness of abandonment palpable, and I closed my eyes and prayed: *Please, please, please, if Michael is angry, please let him forgive me.*

There were pages and pages of links to hopeful adoptive parents' profiles, but after briefly viewing a handful, I avoided them. The combination of their desperation and blatant disregard for first parents' grief made my stomach churn.

I also searched for books about adoption reunions for first-parents, wanting to explore the experience more in-depth but was disappointed to find none. Nothing at the library. Nothing online. The empathy I felt for other women navigating the fallout of adoption gave me new insight. Although I didn't find a formula for a happy reunion, I decided I needed to follow my gut, listen to people I respected, and proceed with compassion for myself as well as for Michael. Two days later, a reply came from Michael, and I couldn't open the message fast enough.

> *Hey,*
> *Everything is going pretty good; school has been a little hectic, but I think I'm going to make it. I have some senior pictures. If you want me to send them to you, just give me your address.*

> *Oh my Goddess, yes, I would love that! But, damnit! I already gave you my address!* I couldn't stop my knee-jerk reaction. *Did you forget? Did you even read my previous email?*

> *How is the weather up there? I have always wanted to go up there, but, of course I don't really have the means to do that right now in my life.*

Oh, how I would love it if you came to visit!

> *I don't know if I'm going to graduate this year… But that's all OK because I will just take classes next year, but in the meantime, I'm going to take a few prep courses at the college I'm going to (MN West), and then next year I will go for half of the day to high school, and the rest will be online classes or something, so I think I've got it all planned out.*
> *Sequentially Yours,*
> *Michael*

Sequentially? What the hell does that mean?

Reading the letter felt as if Michael was holding me at arm's length, as if he were treating me like an unusual rock, trying to decide whether to take a closer look, put me in his pocket, or toss me aside.

I resolved not to write back right away, out of spite, and to give myself time to process.

Then, surprisingly, I got a letter from David three days later.

Hi Candace,

I hope all is well with you guys. We are getting ready for graduation. Michael is missing an elective credit, and so he needs to do some things to satisfy his senior requirements. Not a big deal as he needs to do an online class from Worthington Community College, and he will meet his high school requirements. I am proud of him for making the strides he did this year as he is a smart kid, and once he decided he wanted to get his poop together, he found he could be successful.

I couldn't help but chuckle at "poop."

He has been accepted at Worthington, a school in Minnesota that he wanted to attend as it had a computer course that was what he wanted.

I know that Michael has been thinking of you, and he is happy to know things are good for you.

Take care, Dave and Lori

Any communication from David or Michael was welcome, but why now? Did Michael mention to David I'd written? Or that he'd written to me? Was he concerned I hadn't written back yet? Did it matter?

"There's no way to know," Tom said. "You need to remember, actually keep in the forefront of your mind," he tapped his forehead, "that Michael is a teenage boy. You are not, and will not be, his priority, no matter how much you wish you were. I'm sorry, but that's just how it is."

I sat on the opposite end of the couch, tears rolling down my cheeks. "Yeah," I choked.

"I know this is hard and not the way you wish it were playing out, but he'll come around. It may not be today, tomorrow, or even next year, but he will eventually want to connect with you." Tom reached over and lay his open hand between us on the couch. I placed mine in his. "Give him time to mature." He paused momentarily, then asked, "Did you find any more good information online today?"

"Not really, but I read some more blogs. I'm lucky, actually. There are a lot of adoptees who don't even want to reunite. At least I have that."

"Good, that's what you need to do; look on the bright side."

I snorted. "That's what I'm trying to do."

"I love you, and you're amazing." He caressed my hand while we talked. "Someday, you and Michael will have a great relationship. You'll see."

I moved to get up, his hand still in mine. "I love you too. I'm gonna work on a reply. Take a look when I'm done?"

"Of course. And call my mom. She will totally understand. I never called her when I was Michael's age. Besides, she loves it when you look to her for advice and support."

Hi Mike,

Sounds like you've got things pretty well in hand and a plan for the future. There are no rules that say you have to do things the same way everyone else does them. What's important is figuring out what it is you want to do and how you're planning to do it, and there's not really a timeline in how long it should take you to get there. As for school, I did okay (not great) in high school, then bombed out of college my first year and didn't go back until after you were born. I'm glad I finally went to college and got my degree, although I don't use it like it was meant to be used. I think college gave me some much-needed confidence-building experiences and a chance to grow up a bit, as well as some skills.

And yes, I would very much like one of your senior photos, if you have any available. And I am still interested in seeing your book as well. Here's my address.

Take care and happy spring.

Candace

I gave him my address again but purposefully left out any term of endearment. No matter how hard I tried to feel grateful, I was upset that he didn't seem to want to pursue a relationship and bitter that I had no control to change it. I also didn't expect him to send a graduation picture or his book because I finally accepted the truth of Tom's words: I was the furthest thing from his mind.

CHAPTER 17

Six Months Later—November 2008
18 Years Old

A tiny bell over the door chimed as Julie and I entered the coffee shop. The aroma of cinnamon and nutmeg buffeted us along with the warm, moist air inside. We stomped our boots on the entrance mat to dislodge clinging snow, and then sidled up to the counter.

Julie and I met about twice a month to chat, which usually consisted of half business and half pleasure. She owned the gallery I'd worked at since Tom and I came to Skagway more than ten years before, and she'd become a close friend. Two years my senior, she had three children, one close in age to Michael, and knew more about my struggles with our reunion than anyone other than Tom.

"I still haven't heard anything from Michael," I told her after we settled. "Right now, I plan to reach out for Christmas. I'll let him know we're in the state, and maybe, just maybe, I'll get the chance to see him."

"That would be so wonderful," Julie took a sip of her chai latte. "So, what's your final plan for this winter?"

"I told you that Tom's sister, Kim, bought a house in central Minnesota and moved there from Arizona, right?"

She nodded. Strands of her long, blond hair stuck up in a fuzzy crown from static electricity.

"Well, we're going to invest in a small piece of adjoining land. It's already got a year-round cabin on it, so we'll reside there during the winter months, and other relatives can use it in the summer. We like the idea of being closer to family, and it will be an excellent fallback in case things don't work out here."

"And I'm sure being closer to Michael, just in case he wants to meet, is a serious bonus." Her blue eyes sparkled and crinkled at the corners.

"Yeah," I said, feeling like a child counting down the days until Christmas. "I would love it if we started regularly getting together in the winter. Maybe he might even want to come to stay with us for a while."

Back in Minnesota, the months of November and December passed in a flurry. We transformed the cabin from a bunk-style one-room shack into a cozy cottage, complete with a modern kitchen and bathroom, including running water.

"Anything from Michael?" Tom leaned in behind me to see the computer screen, then rested his chin on the top of my head.

"Nope, not a thing." I sighed. Christmas and New Year's had come and gone without any response from Michael to our latest email. There was nothing I could do, and I needed to accept it. "I'm okay, though. I think. I mean, I'm disappointed, yes, but at least I know he's doing well."

"Has there been anything new on his MySpace?" His voice resonated through my skull.

"Not for almost three months."

"Well, that sucks." He stood abruptly. "I'm sorry."

I was in the dark, but unlike before, at least I knew he was okay, and I trusted David would alert me to any problems. The connections I'd made with first parents and adoptees all advised taking things slowly. And since the adoptee was the only member of the adoption triad—first parent, adoptive parent, adoptee—who had zero influence when the placement happened, I agreed that Michael needed to have control of the pace and development of our relationship.

"Well," I shook my head, "let's get to work then. What's the schedule for today?"

We were completing the construction of a dual workshop next to the cabin. Tom's mechanical engineering background enabled him to design, fix, and troubleshoot just about everything, and I was a willing and capable helping hand. I found a great deal of satisfaction in our combined skills and teamwork. Plus, I was grateful for the mental and physical distractions.

"We finished putting up the sheetrock yesterday," he said, switching into supervisor mode, "so you can start mudding and taping today while I begin installing outlets. But first, why don't you go for a ski? The snow that fell last night is perfect. I'll run to town to rent a movie for tonight, and when I get back, we'll get started."

Some evenings, we trudged the trampled path next to the fenced-in pasture over to Tom's sister's place to play pinochle or Rock Band with our niece and nephew. Other nights, we snuggled on the bed with Luna between us and read or pulled out our guitars and noodled around. The peace and quiet of rural living suited me fine. I loved our sunrise coffee hour, gazing out the double-deck doors at the horses in the paddock, their nostrils spewing great white plumes.

But the remainder of the winter passed without any communication from Michael.

The following spring, back in Skagway, Tom took me to the annual Mother's Day Brunch, where I prided myself in hardly crying at all. Michael hadn't written since *last* Mother's Day, but I focused on the fact that my son was okay. And with Tom's support and encouragement, I tentatively began to share Michael's existence with friends and acquaintances.

In July, for the third year in a row, I participated in what had become my favorite annual volunteer activity: being a clown for the Fourth of July Parade. I'd acquired an adorable costume: a hoop-bottomed, multicolored baby doll dress, a bright orange curly wig with a bonnet, pink tights, and bunny slippers. I loved how my inhibitions vanished when I donned the makeup and costume. No one knew who I was or had any expectations. I became an entirely different person. Someone whimsical and frivolous. Free to cartwheel, skip, hop, and hug strangers. This person, who danced beneath a Barbie umbrella and wore a big red nose, made people smile. And I loved her for it.

Over the summer and through the fall, I talked about Michael more frequently, dismantling my protective barricade. And when people mentioned their children at parties, I chimed in for the first time.

"I have a son," I'd say, reciting almost verbatim the same lines while my face beamed. "I placed him for adoption as a baby, and he contacted me when he turned eighteen."

Shocked facial expressions from longtime acquaintances morphed into delighted nods and "oh, that's wonderful" and "how exciting." Only a select few close friends knew about Michael until this point. When they invariably asked me to tell them more, my chest would swell with pride.

"He's your average teenage boy who likes video games and has a girlfriend. I haven't met him yet but hope he will want to. I'm letting him call the shots."

When I first began to open up, I was often awkward and tearful and halting but always forthright. Usually, people shared my excitement about our future relationship then launched into a story about an aunt who gave her baby away or a cousin who was adopted. Everyone seemed to have an adoption story. But sometimes those stories were not happy—a first mother who wouldn't reconnect or an adoptee whose adoptive family was abusive—and the looks of dismay, and even hatred, triggered old internal messages of shame.

"I'm sorry. I didn't mean to bring up a difficult subject," I'd say and walk away, unable to withstand the reproachful stares. And I *was* sorry. I didn't want to cause anyone distress, but my bravery in speaking up was helping build self-acceptance, so I continued to share despite judgmental reactions.

In early November, Tom and I headed back to Minnesota. With our workshop complete, we could immerse ourselves in creative activities. Although a wall divided the interior space, to keep Tom's wood dust from infiltrating my silversmithing zone, we shared a sound system, which enabled us to listen to audiobooks during the day and then chat about them over dinner.

"Since we haven't heard anything from Michael," I said at dinner one night in mid-December. "How about I send an email to David instead?"

"Good idea. David will write back, I'm sure."

I thought so too, but I also wanted to minimize the potential for disappointment. Silence from David would be less painful than from Michael – or so I thought.

Dec 21, 2009
Hello Dave,
I thought I'd drop a note to you in hopes of finding out if everything is going all right. I have not heard anything from Michael and am unwilling to push contact on him, and I hoped you might be willing to share updated info.
We are well and in Minnesota again for part of the winter. We continue to work on artwork in the winter months and the tourism industry in Skagway for the summers. We will be taking a long saved-for trip to New Zealand and Australia this Feb/March, and we are very excited.
I hope you have a very Merry Christmas and a Happy New Year.
Warm Holiday Wishes,
Candace

The next morning, the scarlet of first light dissolved into tangerine then marigold, culminating in the sun breaking over the horizon like a daffodil, its ray-like petals unfolding across the snow-packed meadow. Tom and I sipped coffee and watched the horses meander in the pasture, their long tails swishing gracefully, while Luna lay on her tummy in the middle of the room, holding a rawhide stick between her paws and chewing loudly.

"All right, grab the laptop," Tom said. "I know you're dying to see if David wrote back."

I was. So far, David had always responded quickly to our correspondences, and I hoped that hadn't changed. When I saw his name in the inbox, tension I didn't realize I'd been holding drained from my shoulders. And, like two years before, I devoured the update.

Candace,
Nice to hear from you and that things are going well for you. Everything is going well here. Michael is going to school at Southwest State University in Marshall starting in January. He is pretty excited about this. Lori, my wife, and I are also pretty excited as we will then be empty nesters for the first time.

Oh. Yeah. I hadn't thought about it like that. The fact that Michael is old enough to connect with me means he's also old enough to leave you.

Michael and Hannah are heading to Minneapolis this weekend for Christmas Eve.

I'm so glad they're still together.

I am hoping they get stranded here because of the projected snowstorm, so they have to spend Christmas Eve with us.

I smiled. *So I'm not the only one who wants to have him around.*

I had asked Michael if he had any correspondence with you a few times and he had said he hadn't but that he had over 5,000 emails that he had not opened.

What? Seriously? The skin on the back of my neck bristled.

He said he was going to work on getting this cleaned up so he could check. I will let him know you had sent him something to his email as I know that he would be very happy to hear from you. If you do not hear anything, please do not hesitate to contact me.

Oh good. I didn't want to overstep any boundaries.

Take care of yourselves, and have a very blessed Holiday Season.
With our love,
David

Later that same day, he sent a post-script.

Candace,
I talked to Michael a bit ago, and he was excited to hear that you had contacted me. He is going to try to send you an email this afternoon.
David

I wasn't sure how to respond to this. I wanted to be happy and was, initially, then reigned in my excitement.

"I just wonder if it's real. I mean, could David be sugar-coating it?" I asked Tom as I looked at the email. "Could Michael be like 'no big deal' but David is trying to soften the blow?"

"I suppose, but I'm guessing things just got lost between the cracks. Remember, he's a teenager. I'd encourage you to approach this at face value and quit trying to read into it. Okay?"

"Yeah, okay. I will." So, I permitted myself to feel hopeful an email was imminent.

And then, two days later, after nearly two years without a word, Michael wrote.

Dec 24, 2009
Sorry for not responding to anything you may have sent; I don't really do the whole email thing.

You've got to be joking? You were the one who wanted to use email! Then I gasped.

Is it true you're in Minnesota? If so, we should try and get together, if that's cool with you.

I sprang to my feet, leaned over, and put my face right in front of the computer screen.

Shoot me back an email, and I promise to check for it. SEP *Mike*

"He wants to meet!" I squealed, rushing over to Tom.

"Oh, that's great, sweetie. I know you've been hoping for this." He gave me a quick one-armed squeeze. "Write him back and let him know we're available pretty much anytime. What a great Christmas present, huh?"

I took a slow breath and held it. A tiny voice in the back of my mind worried about things going awry, but I couldn't help but smile as I forced the air out of my lungs.

Finally.

A rapid-fire dialogue, via email, ensued.

Dec 25, 8:36 AM
Hi Mike,
It's very good to hear from you. Yes, I am in Minnesota and would very much like to get together. My schedule is flexible, so let me know what might work for you. If you'd rather text than email, I'm okay with that too.
Merry Christmas
Candace

Dec 25, 2:28 PM
I'm good for anything. I'll be home in like a day or two, so sometime after that. How long are you going to be here? Are you anywhere near Marshall?
Mike

Dec 26, 9:20 AM
We will be in MN for another month.
We are just north of Little Falls, about three and a half hours north of Marshall.
I talked with Tom, and we are going to be free the Saturday after New Year, Jan. 2.
Is that too soon after the busy holidays?
Candace

Dec 26, 9:58 AM
Hmm, I'm sure that will work, but I'll check to make sure. Would it be better for me to drive there or for you to come here? I'm up for whatever.
Mike

Dec 27, 7:38 AM
No problem for us to drive there, and if that day doesn't work, let me know.
Candace

In the end, after more than two dozen messages over two weeks, we finally set a date.

"Oh my God, I thought we'd never figure it out," I plopped down on a wood stump in Tom's workshop. My body sagged as if I'd just run a marathon.

"Great! When?"

"Next Saturday."

He smiled, pulled me to my feet, and gave me a big hug. "I'm so happy for you. For us!"

On Thursday, two days until the reunion, I went skiing. I'd gone frequently after our arrival in Minnesota and every day since setting a date for our meeting.

Goddess, it's beautiful out here. The stillness and shimmering snow cover created a fantasyland-like haven, punctuated by the *swish-swish* of my skis and the occasional daytime *hoot-hoot* of a snowy owl. I crisscrossed the 160-acre homestead for over an hour, up and down hillocks and over frozen ponds, while the wind slipped between birch and oak trees to kiss my face.

When I get back, I will finish the setting for the opal pendant, then draw a ring design for that stunning chrysoprase cabochon. I might have to keep that one... Although I was nervous and excited for the upcoming meeting, I worked industriously and intently in my workshop every day. I gleaned immense satisfaction when the metal's luster emerged at the touch of the buffing wheel: that moment, each one-of-a-kind piece sprang to life.

And tonight, we'll work on "Grantchester Meadows." Tom's almost perfected the first guitar part, so we'll have it if I can just get the vocals down. Tom and I usually played games with his sister, niece, and nephew in the evenings, but we'd been staying in the cabin for the last week, playing guitar and learning new songs. This Pink Floyd song had been one of our favorites back when we were hanging out in high school, and the sorrowful melody coupled with the hopeful lyrics suited my current mood nicely.

Icy wind of night, be gone
This is not your domain
In the sky a bird was heard to cry
Misty morning whisperings and gentle stirring sounds
Belied a deathly silence that lay all around
Hear the lark and harken to the barking of the dog fox gone to ground
See the splashing of the kingfisher flashing to the water

And a river of green is sliding unseen beneath the trees
Laughing as it passes through the endless summer making for
the sea

When the day of the reunion arrived, I awoke early but skipped our regular sunrise coffee hour and instead carried the steaming cup into the bathroom. After my shower, I swiped moisture from the mirror and stared into my eyes, noting the unusually thick black ring that circled my irises.

I'll have to check if Michael's are like that too.

I lathered lavender-scented lotion all over, then applied my foundation.

I wonder if he's as excited and nervous as I am. What will he think of me?

Brow pencil next, then mascara, using a dulled safety pin to separate the clumpy lashes.

Does he even know what I look like?

Although we had stalked Michael's MySpace, we had no way of knowing if he'd ever even looked at ours. And he hadn't posted anything new to his page in over a year.

Will he look different?

The occasional whiff of burnt hair drifted through the tiny room as I used the blow-dryer. I'd always considered my fiery mane to be my best feature, and I wanted it to be perfect.

It wasn't.

I'd recently started greying at the temples, so I'd dyed it in preparation for this meeting, but the color was still a bit too fresh for my liking. *Oh well, it'll have to do.*

I'd thought about what I would wear for days, hoping to find the right balance between a hip, mature adult and a sensible mother figure. I decided on slim, boot-cut jeans, a blue and grey knitted sweater, black boots, and a belt. A Celtic pendant I'd made showed prominently at my throat with matching earrings.

Tom peeked over the laptop frequently with the corners of his mouth lifting. "I love watching you get ready, but today more than ever. You're kind of glowing, actually."

As we drove to Marshall, blustery late-January winds blew light, dry snow across the two-lane highway and blocked out the weak sunlight. Random blasts of wind buffeted the truck's driver side and forced Tom to concentrate, wary of black ice. Neither of us spoke.

I fidgeted in the passenger seat, alternating sitting stock-straight and slouching down.

Will he be happy to meet me?

I pulled off my boots and placed both stocking feet on the dashboard, then sat back up, then crossed and uncrossed my legs a dozen times.

What if he doesn't like me?

Staring out the window, I counted telephone poles in sets of three as they slipped by. Smoke from farmhouses, drawn horizontal by the winds, created stripes in the sky. I lost count.

What if he's changed his mind?

The wind gusted like the questions and concerns that swirled through my mind. Sighing, I sank my fingers in Luna's long hair as she slept on a pillow between us, her nose buried in the curl of her tail.

What if he's angry? What if he doesn't want to meet me?

As the miles slipped by, negativity spread like bacteria in a culture. An invisible battle raged inside. I almost convinced myself Michael and David would turn us away at the door. Then, I shook my head to dispel the darkness and decided I needed to accept whatever happened. If he were angry, he would have a chance to tell me to my face. I could take it.

Hell, I deserved it anyway.

"You okay?" Tom asked.

"Yeah, just dealing with some negative self-talk over here," I admitted. "I'll be okay."

"All right," He paused, then added, "And just a cautionary note: You know how you always say you don't regret your decision to place Michael for adoption?"

"Yeah?"

"I'm pretty sure you say that to convince yourself most of the time, but don't say that to him." He stared straight ahead.

I shivered. I'd never thought how that would sound to an adopted child, and I suddenly realized how cruel those words would be. I'd said it many times. I'd even said it around other adoptees. My gut roiled again.

The next thing I knew, we turned into a residential neighborhood. Tiny beads of sweat broke out along my hairline, and my mouth went dry. The truck crept along the winding street through a community filled with beautiful homes, their expansive lawns covered in pristine blankets of snow while treetops swayed above.

My breaths came faster as we parked along the curb of a cul-de-sac. I waited for Tom to open his door—I didn't want to be first. Then, I stepped out with Luna in my arms. I set her down to pee next to a snow berm, and once she'd gone, I put her back in the truck, with plans to check on her frequently.

Tom met me at the back of the truck, where we joined gloved hands and turned toward the driveway – I wished I could feel his skin against mine. My heart beat staccato in the hollow of my throat and whooshed inside my hood, creating a rhythmic tune only I could hear. Our footsteps left impressions in the snow as we stepped onto the unshoveled walkway to the front door, and as we neared, two tall, broad men stepped out onto the landing: David, with Michael right behind.

CHAPTER 18

February 2, 2010
20 Years Old

My heart did a somersault. Michael stood on the doorstep, smiling. I felt my cheeks lift, and I think my lips reached my ears.

He'd put on weight since the last photo I'd seen, and I almost tripped, noting how much he resembled David. It was uncanny.

As Tom and I approached the door, David engulfed me in a warm embrace without hesitation. As soon as he let go, I turned to Michael, my tongue thick with emotion, "Can I hug you?"

He opened his arms.

I think I teleported myself to him because suddenly I was lost in his embrace. Part of me felt like a little girl, unsure how to act or what to do. I struggled to reconcile that this tall, robust man was my little boy and that I was the adult and he the child. My body felt tingly and effervescent, my mind as if I'd drunk a bottle of champagne. I thought I might float away.

I focused on details to keep myself grounded to the earth. His hair was dishwater blond with golden highlights in a shaggy bowl-cut. He had a nose ring, stretched ear lobes with big plugs, and acne. He wore a red-and-black plaid shirt which, along with his lumberjack body, reminded me of the School House Rock song about adjectives: a big man can have a boyish face.

A low hum, like a honeybee on a bright summer day, rose from somewhere deep inside and took up residence in my rib cage: part sound, part sensation, it intensified until it filled my body with a thousand bees. My senses seemed heightened, but I also felt numb.

I followed them inside and absently handed David my jacket, and the next thing I knew, we were in a spacious dining room. Artificial light from a wide chandelier augmented the weak wintertime daylight from the floor-to-ceiling windows. Tom and David exchanged small talk while Michael and I glanced at each other nervously.

I wanted to reach over and pull him to me, to hold his head against my buzzing chest and feel his breath sync with mine. To never let him go. But I didn't want to scare him. Instead, I tucked my hands into the sleeves of my sweater and cradled myself. The bees buzzed and hummed, buzzed and hummed.

The thump of a ceramic cup on the table broke the spell.

"Did you want cream?" David asked.

Even though I like milk in my coffee, I shook my head, both to decline the offer and to disperse the bees.

"So, are you my birth father?" Michael blurted to Tom, and as if a door slammed, the buzzing stopped.

"No," Tom and I replied in unison.

Haven't we covered this already via email? Maybe he never read it.

"No," Tom repeated. "But I saw Candace when she was pregnant."

His easy tone made me swivel my head toward him. *Does he know how off-balance I feel?* With the bees gone, I felt like I was floating away again.

"She was about eight months along. It was almost Christmas. I felt you move in her tummy, actually."

Ah...my cue. I nodded. "Tom was one of the few people who touched my belly when I was carrying you." I was so glad he shared this tidbit of information. I wanted Michael to like Tom.

"Oh. Okay. Do you have any brothers or sisters?" Michael asked.

"Yes." His quick switch of topic surprised me. I thought he'd want more information about his first father, but I was glad because I didn't have any to offer. "I have four siblings: two sisters and two brothers."

"Cool. I'd like to meet them sometime," he leaned forward expectantly. "Especially your brothers."

Thrilled at the possibility, the bees returned. The humming now accompanied by pressure, like the swarm straining to break free.

"Michael has five sisters but only one brother," David explained. "And tons of nieces but no nephews." A gentle smile spread across his face, rounder than when I'd first met him, but his blue eyes still held kindness. "I think he feels a little overloaded by the estrogen levels in this house." He reached over and playfully scuffed Michael's hair.

"Maybe," I directed my answer to Michael, "we could have a family gathering, and you could come to St. Cloud?" Plans had already begun to take shape in the back of my mind.

"That sounds cool."

After about half an hour, Tom got up from the table. "I'm going to go out and check on Luna. I'll be right back."

"Why don't you bring her in the house?" David asked.

I leaned back in my chair and sighed with relief but immediately refocused on Michael.

He entranced me. I couldn't keep up with the conversation as it continued, Luna now on my lap. This boy, on the cusp of manhood, tall yet still soft around the edges, was wondrous. Heat suffused my whole body. *Pride?* And, oh, the similarities. His hands looked and moved like mine, ruddy and thick, punctuating his words with dramatic flair. His lips, like mine, were plump when in rest but thinned when he talked. And naturally dark red. *Women will be jealous.* That lick of hair, above his right temple, angled just a little off by the cowlick: mine.

Michael and David leaned toward each other as they spoke, and I sensed mutual love and respect. And although I could see myself in Michael, he was like David, too. It was fascinating to witness the parallels in their mannerisms, body language, and speech styles. Once, they both placed an elbow on the table simultaneously, a mirror of each other. In that room, nature and nurture were on full display.

Over the next two hours, we chit-chatted about grandparents and cousins, family health and illnesses, and high school shenanigans.

"Last winter, I shoveled snow all around the neighborhood, wearing my kilt," Michael said. "*Only* my kilt." He smirked at David.

"I've got a picture of it, actually." David chuckled. "Hey, let's move to the other room and look at the photo albums!"

My shoulder brushed up against Michael's arm as we moved through the doorway, kicking up the bees again.

I can't wait to see these.

After David switched on the light over the formal dining room table, he pulled out a stack of albums, sifting through to find the early years. The pictures, and their related stories, complemented those I'd received when Michael was growing up and filled in the missed years. Of course, there were pictures of Jane, but they didn't refer to her absence, and I didn't ask. How could I when resentment still seethed inside me?

Why can't you let it go? What are you so afraid of?

And suddenly, I knew that Jane and I were the same.

We both abandoned Michael.

Shame—at judging her and for my own failings—crept under my skin like a slithering snake, and I shivered. I wasn't yet ready to forgive either one of us.

By sheer force of will, I refocused my attention on how Michael's eyes rested on Jane's image. He didn't appear angry or upset. His smooth brow, bright eyes, and laughter signaled he was entirely at ease. Everyone seemed relaxed. We laughed and joked about funny clothes and out-of-fashion glasses.

Has Michael forgiven Jane? The buzzing, which had muted at my sudden distress, softly rose again.

Maybe. And maybe, he will forgive me too. I eased back, and my body melted into the upholstered chair.

In no hurry for the day to end, Tom and I readily agreed to join Michael and David for a late lunch at a local café. Bright red vinyl seats and big, tri-fold color menus greeted us as we slid into the booth, knocking over a tower of single-serving half-and-half cups. Michael ordered coffee, added ice cubes, and gulped it down, requesting a refill right away.

I had a fleeting worry about the caffeine. *Hm. Is this parental protectiveness?*

David didn't seem concerned, so I followed his lead.

Casual conversation flowed. Michael became chattier, using big words and projecting a maturity he did not yet possess. *Is he trying to impress me?* Tom and I held hands under the table while David draped his arm casually behind Michael's back.

A man wearing blue jeans, a flannel button-up shirt, and a Minnesota Twins baseball cap stopped at the table. "Hi David, Michael, how're things?"

"Lester! Good to see you." David shook his hand. Both he and Michael smiled. "We're doing great! This is Candace and Tom. Candace is Michael's birth mother."

I twitched back, shoulder blades flat against the booth-back. "Hi," was all I could say.

"They're visiting from Alaska." David turned to us, "Lester worked with me at Archer Daniels Midland for a few years."

I didn't hear what else they said. David's open and easy acceptance of my place in the adoption stunned me and completely contradicted my years-long tendency to view my role in it negatively. By the end of lunch, David had introduced me as Michael's birth mother three times. At each mention, Michael merely nodded his head and smiled.

Years earlier, when Tom first suggested celebrating Michael's birthday, I'd thought he was crazy. He'd slowly convinced me to reframe my perspective and embrace the beauty of Michael's existence, but I'd done so only with Tom. Now I saw firsthand from the other side. The love, acceptance, and pride that flowed from David, along with everything else I'd witnessed, fed the growing respect and love I felt for him.

Back at the house, we sat at the long kitchen counter, a plate of homemade oatmeal-raisin cookies perched at one end. Michael shared his enthusiasm for computers, using words and terminology I didn't know and couldn't comprehend. But I laughed, my feet hooked on the bar stool foot rail, shoulders relaxed.

"Hey, let's take some pictures." Tom stood and pulled his phone from his breast pocket.

"Great idea," David said. "Let's go into the living room."

I jumped up, then replaced my chair slowly to cover my elation.

"Okay, Michael and Candace, stand in front of the fireplace," David directed. "Yeah, right there."

I sidled up next to Michael, turned my body toward him, and leaned in while David and Tom prepared. He smelled like a mix of Axe body spray and body odor, slightly sweet and acidic. Covertly, I inhaled.

Tom and David alternately encouraged us to look their way, and, posed with an arm around each other, we smiled on cue. The sheer bliss on my face is captured for posterity.

Eventually, Tom joined us, and Luna too. A sweet family portrait.

"Let's email copies to each other, okay?" David suggested.

"I would love that, thank you," I said.

I felt as though I was bobbing in a hot tub: cloyingly warm and buoyant as if the bubbles were bursting around me in celebration. I'd done everything I'd wanted: hugged and held my son, listened to stories, and learned history. I even had photographs of us together. After five hours, my body ached, and my thoughts blurred. Although I yearned to stay in that afternoon forever, I also wanted to release it at the perfect moment.

Abruptly, I walked to the entryway closet, opened it, and pulled out my coat. "All right. We're going to go."

"Um," Tom raised his eyebrows, "Yeah, okay."

I slipped my boots on, then picked up Luna. Tom was still standing there, mouth open.

"Ah, can I go start the truck?" I didn't answer, just looked at him blankly. He threw on his boots and jacket and slipped out the door.

"Maybe we can try to arrange a small gathering with my brothers next month, after our vacation," I suggested, trying to fill what was now becoming awkward silence. "How does that sound?"

"Sure, sounds good." Michael nodded. "Your trip to Australia sounds cool."

"Yes, I hope you have a great vacation," David added. "And drive carefully heading home."

Tom returned, stomped his boots on the rug, then I handed him Luna. I turned to Michael. "Today has been wonderful. I can't tell you how happy it has made me to see your face and hug you." I embraced him, choking back tears, then, to David, added, "Thank you for being such a good dad and sharing him with me." I reached out to him for a hug, too. "This has been perfect." One last time, I grabbed Michael around the neck. I kissed his cheek, then whispered, "I love you."

Michael didn't say anything, but he put his arms around me and squeezed. Tears flowed freely down my cheeks as I walked out the door.

"That was a pretty abrupt departure," Tom said as we climbed into the still cold, stiff truck. "Are you okay?"

"Yeah." The moisture on my cheeks stung in the frigid air. "Just overwhelmed, I guess. It was such a beautiful day. I didn't want to spoil it by blubbering all over the place."

"Oh, okay," he shrugged and threw the truck in gear.

Luna shook her coat out and settled on her pillow before we'd cleared the neighborhood.

"So?" He cocked his head.

"Amazing." I breathed and reached over Luna to squeeze his arm through his bulky jacket. "I'm gonna need a little time to digest, though."

I stared out the window without seeing anything.

My son.

Then, feeling warmth and solidarity with David, I amended my thought: *Our son.*

David had done what I wanted and hoped: raised a boy to be a man, a caring, sensitive, creative human being. Gratitude overwhelmed me.

Throughout the drive home, I oscillated between tears of joy over our meeting and sadness that it was over.

"I hope we can see him again after we get back from our trip."

"Yes." Tom smiled indulgently. "You're gleaming, you know." He seemed just as happy as me.

The following day, I emailed Michael and David to thank them for welcoming us. I also apologized for the abrupt departure and mentioned the meeting with my brothers. Michael responded the very next day.

I had a good time too, so did Dave. I understand you having to leave and understand that emotions were running high.

I'm up for getting together anytime it's possible. I think it would be really neat to get to know everyone, or at least meet them. But we have plenty of time to figure things out.

Mike

And I agreed. Plenty of time.

As we prepared to travel to Australia, I dreamt about a future with Michael. Nothing was off-limits. Family holidays and birthday parties. Concerts and visits to the science museum. Even trips for him to Alaska.

Once overseas, I wrote small vignettes of our travels, sending them out via mass email to friends and family. Everything I wrote, though, was really for Michael. I wanted him to know what we were doing and the fun we were having. I hoped he'd want to travel with us someday. Now that he had met us, I was confident we'd turned a corner in our relationship, and things would become more interactive.

On our arrival back in the U.S., we had less than two weeks in Minnesota before returning to Alaska for work. I tried to arrange a get-together with Michael and my brothers, but nothing materialized. Michael had a busy social life, which surpassed the desire to meet his birth uncles. I didn't worry; we would get the chance next fall. Everything would be different now that we'd met. We would build a relationship, learn about each other, and spend time together.

The world was our oyster.

CHAPTER 19

Two Weeks Later—February 2010
20 Years Old

"I'm so excited about our future with Michael," I said to Tom as we drove through Alberta, Canada, back to Alaska. Neither the colorless snow-swept landscape nor the negative thirteen-degree temperature could quash my hopefulness. I swiveled toward him, eyebrows raised, grinning girlishly. "This fall, I'll set up a family gathering for him to meet Miles and Bobby, and maybe Stacy will even drive up from Missouri."

"Don't get too far ahead of yourself. You've got to remember he's just a kid. Now that he's met you, he probably won't even think about you for a while."

My shoulders sagged, and I faced forward again. *Why can't he just be excited? Or at least let me be for a little while?*

When we got to Skagway, I printed all the photos of Michael and me, framed my favorite, and placed it prominently on the entertainment center. Then, humming softly, I tucked the one with me, Michael, Tom, and Luna into my wallet. With permission, Tom posted all of them on our Facebook page, with the glaring message: *For those of you who didn't know who Mike is...Well, Candace met her son Mike for the first time yesterday. Twenty years after he was adopted...It was a wonderful day...~tom.*

From February through June, we communicated primarily by text at his request. I sent quick messages like "How're things going?" or "Thinking about you and hoping you're doing good," and he replied with, "Doin' great," or "All's well." Each time the text chime sounded, I jumped to find my phone.

It wasn't much, but I couldn't expect him to want to connect with me all the time.

In June, Tom discovered JibJab.

"What's that?"

"A digital entertainment platform. Here, look."

I pulled up a chair, coffee mug in hand, ready to settle in.

"I can personalize an animated video by putting our faces on it." He smirked at me as he played a Star Wars-themed musical skit.

I almost spit out my coffee. He'd pasted my face over Princess Leah's, Michael's on Luke Skywalker, and his own on Han Solo. He even added Luna as Chewy. "That's hilarious."

"I know, right?"

"Michael will love it."

Michael wrote back immediately, "lol"ing and offering to send us some photos of him and Hannah from prom. I bounced through the house. *Prom! His high school romance!* But after a month, my enthusiasm waned. Day after day, I checked email and went to the post office only to discover bills and advertisements, but no photos.

In August, dreaming of getting together in the fall, I emailed him the dates we'd be in Minnesota. *Maybe another day-long visit? Or the theater?* He'd shared his love of performance art when we'd met. I researched upcoming live plays and concert offerings in the Twin Cities, thinking of inviting Michael and Hannah to join us. *Or perhaps a day at the science museum?*

On our drive from Alaska to Minnesota in October, we traveled an extra two hundred miles to go through Marshall, with hopes of seeing him. But Michael was too busy. I sulked for over an hour. Tom chalked it up to bad luck and stopped to buy me an ice cream cone, noticing my sullenness.

"Try not to fixate on it," he said. "It's not like we'd arranged it ahead of time."

By November, I'd made multiple unsuccessful attempts to arrange a get-together with Michael and my brothers. I'd offered to drive to Marshall or meet him and Hannah in the Twin Cities. Finally, Tom put an end to it.

"Give it a rest, okay. Let him come to you. He knows we're here and available anytime he wants. That's all you can do."

I clenched my jaw and let the topic drop.

"By the way, I've asked your dad to come hunt with me. I'm hoping he'll stay for dinner a few nights too."

"And probably a dozen games of cribbage, I'd imagine." Although I still hadn't learned how to communicate with my birth father, I was glad Tom enjoyed his company—it kind of took me off the hook. When they played cards or fished or hunted, I could go off and do my own thing.

"I'm so proud of your willingness to include him in our life." Tom smiled. "I know it's hard sometimes, but he's a good guy. He just got the short end of the stick."

Tom had been adamant that I develop a relationship with my dad. When I learned of his existence at thirteen years old, I'd just been relieved that Gene wasn't my real father—I didn't care that I had a different one. As a teen and young adult, I'd rarely had opportunities to see or speak with my dad. Then I married Tom, and with his encouragement, we started to build a relationship. This was when I discovered that my dad had been tricked into signing away his parental rights. Gene had forced my real dad out and then adopted me. This knowledge had softened my attitude toward my dad, but I still harbored resentment that he hadn't tried harder to reach me, especially after Mom had split from Gene.

This was one reason I tried so hard to connect with Michael. I didn't want him to think, years down the road, that I hadn't put in the effort.

CHAPTER 20

Four Months Later—March 2011
21 Years Old

❝Let's text Michael and see if he's free this afternoon," Tom said, placing the laptop and power cord in its travel case. "Maybe we can see him on our drive out of Minnesota." The optimism in his voice belied a disappointment we both felt.

I spun from the suitcase to send Michael a message. He responded right away.

"He's available," I squealed. "He said we could meet for lunch at his favorite pub."

We finished packing in record time; I sprinted to load everything in the truck for the seasonal drive back to Alaska.

Three hours later, I messaged Michael to let him know we were half an hour out of Marshall and asked for the restaurant's name. Energy coursed through me. I bounced in the passenger seat as we waited for his response. Five minutes passed, then ten. Finally, twenty minutes later, my phone chimed. He couldn't make it. Something had come up.

I silently handed the phone to Tom and turned to face out the window. Hot, bitter tears streamed down my face.

He said he could meet? Now why can't he? My cheeks burned, and my forehead throbbed. *Is there something wrong? Does he know that this feels so cruel?*

And the negative tapes, those that I'd worked so hard to erase, clicked automatically on and shrieked in my head. *Well, I deserve it anyway. It's only fair. I'd abandoned him; now it was his turn. Payback's a bitch, huh?*

Shame, sadness, anger, frustration – I couldn't tell where one stopped and the other began.

Sometime in early 2012, Michael moved to Madison, Wisconsin, following Hannah to college. I don't know when it happened since we learned through a text after the fact. His texting had become even more sporadic and abbreviated.

As the weeks and months passed, Tom did his best to alleviate my impatience and justify Michael's detachment. I'd grind my teeth and cross my arms but still try to express my gratitude for his insights and patience.

"Michael's young and immature. Let him grow up a bit."

"I know, I know," tears forming in my eyes. "But why can't he just send me a quick note?"

"Young men don't talk to their parents unless they want to do laundry or need money. I went months without talking to my mom when I was his age. It's normal."

Has he changed his mind about wanting to get to know me? Maybe he's angry?

"Just be patient. He *WILL* want to get to know you someday."

And I knew he was right. All the first mother websites said the same thing: It'll happen when they're older. I just needed to remain open and available, but my heart remained heavy.

Then, finally, in May of 2012, over two years after our first face-to-face meeting, he sent this email:

Candace,
Hey how have you been? I was wondering if you have and use Facebook or Twitter. I tried to find you but had no luck. This is my new email btw.
Mike

I jumped up from the computer and called Tom.

"Michael wants to be Facebook friends!"

"That's awesome!" I could hear the smile in his voice.

"He couldn't find me. I'm such an idiot!"

"Send him a friend request, and we'll look at his page together after dinner, okay?"

"Okay. I love you." Immediately I sent Michael a request, then a follow-up email.

Hi Mike,

Really good to hear from you; you made my day! I'm not easy to find on Facebook cause Tom & I share a page with no last names, so I sent you a friend request.

Busy here, but good. Our tourist season is just starting, been playing a lot of music with the band and training for a marathon next month.

How's Wisconsin? And how's life treating you? Fill me in when you get a chance.

Candace

Relief flooded through me. Finally, I had a window into his life again. That evening we snuggled side-by-side in the recliner, the computer on Tom's lap and Luna asleep on mine. Michael sported a nerdy buzz-cut in his recent photos, which I loved, and thick, black-framed glasses. His gauged ears had gone from near 4mm to at least 25mm, and he wore plaid shirts and bow ties in almost every picture. I returned his smile in every image as if he stood right in front of me.

He worked at a group home as a personal care attendant and was learning to contact juggle. A short video showed him rolling a crystal ball back and forth on top of his hands, then along his forearms, the ball never losing contact with his skin. It was mesmerizing. It brought to mind the movie, *Labyrinth*, in which David Bowie displayed this novel talent skillfully. Michael had recently posted that he'd gone to a farmer's market where he juggled for tips.

Images of Margot, their striped cat, dominated his newsfeed, along with memes. Lots of memes.

His posts were intense meandering narratives about lofty topics.

"There is no such thing as a miracle. It's just statistics. Everything that can happen will, and according to quantum mechanics, anything is possible. You can call it a miracle, but that's not what it truly is.

What I mean is that the word 'miracle' is not an accurate de-scription of what most people usually call a miracle. Because what you just described is not a miracle. Anything that can happen will (and anything is possible). If something other than anything hap-pened, I would call it a miracle.

Furthermore, if a god were to perform a miracle, it would only be a miracle from our perspective. The god would understand how to perform such an act, thus removing its miracle status."

"Wow, he's so deep," I said. "And unapologetic, look at that," indicating a bumper sticker that read "Religion, Get Out of Politics Or Be Taxed."

"I like this one," Tom said and pointed to "My Other Car Is A Tardis." Tom is a Dr. Who fan.

Then, a quote from Ed Begley Jr., "I don't understand why when we destroy something created by man we call it **vandalism**, but when we destroy something created by nature we call it **progress**."

Michael's posts revealed an eclectic personality with the heart of a kind, caring young man. He liked a variety of music, thought mar-ijuana should be legal and believed in human rights. I put my hands behind my head and sighed.

I spent hours on Facebook stalking him and learning about his interests. It had been a long time since I could enjoy seeing him anytime I wanted. It was glorious.

"Hey, Michael was on Facebook last night," Tom said early one morning as he got ready for work. "I commented on one of his posts, and he wrote back right away." It was mid-November, and there had been virtually no messages from Michael again for months, other than his short, random replies to my texts. "He was at home, bored, and watching *Star Wars*."

"Oh?" I lifted my head and stiffened my shoulders. I was in the kitchen getting coffee but didn't turn around to look at him. Instead, I grabbed my cup and brushed past him into the living room.

"Hey, what's wrong?"

"I don't know." I did know, though, and turned to face him. "I guess I'm jealous. He'll chat with you, but..."

"Aw, come on. It wasn't a chat, really. I just commented on one of his posts. Besides, he's at that age where he's more likely to want to talk to another guy. Don't take it too seriously." To-go mug in hand, he asked, "I gotta go, you all right?"

"Yeah, I'm okay." If I said I wasn't, I knew Tom would just repeat his mantra—he's a kid, give him time—and I didn't want to hear it again.

After he left, I logged on to Facebook to read their conversation.

Michael: Spending the evening watching *Star Wars IV, V*, and *VI* while playing with non-Newtonian fluid.

Tom: Love *IV, V, VI* ... hmmm, A Dilatant Oobleck? Or, a Thixotropic Honey? Or a Rheopectic Cream? Or are you just playing with Ketchup? Enjoy the evening.

Michael: Dilatant Oobleck, gotta love corn starch.

That was it. Not much, but still, I bristled.

I don't even know what the heck they're talking about. How am I supposed to connect with him?

I slammed the laptop closed. Although Facebook satisfied my desire for information, I yearned for personal contact. I ached for him to *want* to talk to me, to share his life with me. And I desperately longed to hold him in my arms again.

Consciously, I relaxed my shoulders and blew all the air out of my lungs. *He's almost twenty-three. He's still super young. Quit stressing.*

There's plenty of time.

CHAPTER 21

Thursday—July 4, 2013
23 Years Old

I bunched my hair into a messy bun, and then placed the mobcap over it, but decided not to wear the ruffled neck-liner. It was going to be a hot one.

"You better hurry up; I know how you like to primp at the starting line," Tom yelled from the living room.

"I know, I know, but I've got to get these bunny slippers secured over my shoes first. Last year they flopped around so much I almost tripped a bunch of times."

"Here," he came into the bedroom, "let me help." He bent on one knee and strategically placed pins around the edge of my running sneakers to hold the fuzzy pink fabric in place. "Okay. You look great. I'm sure you'll win the costume award like you always do," he winked.

I'd run the Annual 4th of July Skagway News Runaround in my clown costume for years. Like most running races, there were awards for the fastest runners, but this race also had a prize for best costume. So, given I was adorned in my clown regalia and that I was a seriously slow runner, it's the only award I was sure to win. And, as a bonus, I loved the performance of clowning around at the starting line.

A small crowd had gathered at the News Depot, just three blocks from our house. A folding table was set up on the boardwalk in front of the display window where people completed registration forms, and on the other side of the street, the high school cross-country team warmed up. After I pinned my number onto the front of my outfit,

I sauntered over to the chalk-drawn starting line and lunged into a deeply showy hamstring stretch. Several bystanders barked with laughter while the teenagers shook their heads. Then I bent over and exaggerated trying to reach my toes, which tilted up my hoopskirt, exposing my white ruffled bottom—more chuckles and guffaws from the crowd. I mimed lining up next to two of the serious runners and dramatically nosed my bunny-slippered foot between their Adidas and Asics. The laughter increased as the crowd size grew.

Suddenly, Tom was at my side. He grabbed my arm. "Let's go."

Bewildered, I stared at him and tried to pull away.

He frowned, his complexion ashen. "I have something I need to tell you, just not right here." He latched onto my arm again and practically dragged me along behind him. When we got to the end of the block, I saw Julie striding toward us. I shook my head and tried to dispel the sense of doom. Suddenly, I could barely lift my feet. I yanked from Tom's grasp and stopped.

He hung his head for a split second, and then turned, reaching for my hands. His eyes seemed to sink back into his skull.

"Michael died," he muttered.

"What! What?"

"Michael. He's dead."

I can't...

I crumbled to the ground as if my bones were liquid. A ball of fire in the middle of my chest exploded and pushed lava up my throat and out my mouth, transforming from a blaze into an inhuman freakishly high-pitched wailing screech.

And suddenly, it's like my awareness floated above the scene.

There's a woman... a woman dressed in a clown costume... a clown costume? ... rocking on her knees... wailing.

Am I a banshee? The herald of death?

I can't see her face; her hands cover it. But that sound? What is that sound?

A banshee.

She is too late.

Tom and Julie guided me home. They helped me out of the clown costume and into my robe. I sat on the couch, Luna curled on my lap, her eyes anxiously looking from me to Tom and back again. Julie brought tissues from the bathroom and placed them on the end table next to me. After embracing, she silently left. What was there to say?

I phased in and out of the moment, my body rigid. My mind cycled back over and over: *My son is dead. How is this possible?*

After seeing Julie to the door, Tom called David. I thought Tom said he'd seen a posting on Michael's Facebook page with an RIP post, but I would later discover David had sent an email. I wouldn't read the actual email for another six years.

"David, it's Tom. Can you tell us what happened?" Tom stood quiet in the middle of the room for a long time, then "Okay... When are the services?" Another anxious pause.

Tom glanced in my direction. "I want to go," I silently mouthed. *I have to go...*

"We're going to try to get there. Candace wants to come," his expression hopeful. "Okay, I'll call you back when we know our travel plans. Thank you. And I'm so, so sorry."

"David said he died in his sleep," Tom sat down next to me, slightly askew so he could face me, and reached for my hand. "No sign of why, but they're doing an autopsy. Hannah found him Monday morning." Tom paused. "He said he was sorry for not calling until today."

"Huh? What? Not important. We just need to get there, Tom. I *need* to get there." It never crossed my mind to be upset that David hadn't called right away.

"The viewing is tomorrow, and the funeral is Saturday," Tom slid to the front edge of the couch. "Are you okay? I need to work on getting us out of here." I nodded, and he jumped into action.

"Good morning. My wife and I need to get from Juneau to Minneapolis as soon as possible. There's been a death in the family. Can you help us?" Traveling out of Skagway is difficult in the best of circumstances.

How are we ever going to get there in time? Panic triggered pressure in my chest.

"That's great! What about getting into Minneapolis? No? Well, that's all right. Book us into Seattle." He secured the booking and hung up. "Okay, we'll have to find a connecting flight once we land in Seattle, but that shouldn't be a problem. Now, I'll call Skagway Air. I hope there's room on the ten o'clock." Although the forty-five-minute flight from Skagway to Juneau could be erratic due to weather conditions, the skies were crystal clear.

A silent minute passed, then Tom hung up the phone, worry etched his face. "I got the answering machine. They're not flying today because it's July Fourth." He paced the living room.

"What are we going to do?" The fireball had left my throat raw and swollen.

Tom dialed again. "Robert, this is Tom. You're a pilot, right? Do you have contact info for any of Skagway Air's pilots? We need to get to Juneau." He paused. "We're trying to get to a funeral, and Skag Air's not flying today." Another pause. "Candace's son."

My son is dead?

"Holy crap, Robert, really? Oh man, I can't thank you enough. We'll meet you there in an hour, then. Thank you."

My friends, Kathy, L.C., and Charity, stopped by while I was still in my bathrobe, the frayed edge of its collar clear in my memory, but not their words. Tom must have packed our carry-ons because suddenly we were in a van headed to the airstrip.

Usually, the grandeur of Southeast Alaska and the upper Lynn Canal awed and humbled me while in flight, but I can't remember a thing about that trip.

Two hours later, standing in the departure area of the Juneau airport, I stared out the floor-to-ceiling windows at the 747 we were about to board. It wasn't a full flight—it was the Fourth of July after all—so there weren't many people lining up at Gate Three. I found a secluded corner and pulled out my phone.

"Hi Cand," Mom answered as she usually did. I didn't call her often, nor did she me. Our conversations were always short and to the point.

Suddenly I couldn't find my breath, and her voice changed instantly. "What's wrong?"

Finally, gulping air, I whispered, "Michael... he died."

"What?" Her tone rose an octave.

"Michael. He's dead."

"What are you talking about?" The sudden intensity of her voice, a quality that always signaled the onset of scorn and viciousness, triggered an age-old gut reaction; I shut down. My fight, flight, freeze, or fawn autopilot kicked in.

"I… I… I…" *Why did I call her?* "I guess I thought you should know." I hung up and slumped against the window.

Tom's gentle hands, as if he were handling a crystal figurine, guided me through the gate and steered me down the jetway. He eased me into the window seat, where I folded my arms over my torso and tried to disappear. Tom tucked a handful of tissues into the seatback pocket, then pulled my hand from under my armpit and held it tightly. The stale air was stifling, or perhaps it was just my strained mindset, and when the engines roared at take-off, they mixed with the howl in my soul. Every should-have, could-have, and would-have I'd ever considered since becoming pregnant with Michael bombarded me like a rushing river, the litany of regrets washed over me, and all I could do was sit in the middle of the torrent and hang on.

"We are so fortunate, so very lucky, to have met him when we did," Tom said, right as I was thinking about our first, and only, face-to-face meeting with Michael.

I gaped at him. *Does he know what I'm thinking?* "I know," I choked, then gazed unseeing out the window. *Thank Goddess, I got to hold him in my arms!* Hushed sobs followed.

Then, at the exact moment I was lamenting never having had the chance to watch his favorite television show together, Tom said, "I guess we'll have to watch *Dr. Who* without him."

And when a high-pitched whine began in the back of my throat as I relived the recurring fear that I'd made the wrong choice years ago, Tom turned my face to his and whispered, "Michael had a good life. He was happy and healthy and loved."

Throughout the flight and the days to follow, Tom seemed inexplicably tethered to me, always knowing when and how to comfort me or steer me from self-destructive thoughts. He embodied compassion and tenderness, seldom leaving my side.

Our flight from Juneau got us into Seattle at 5:15 p.m. Tom spoke with the flight attendant as we prepared to land, getting us clearance to move to the front of the disembarking line, then we sprinted to the nearest customer service desk.

"It looks like there's an American Airlines flight at 5:45 p.m. and a Delta at 8:15 p.m.," the agent said as she checked her computer screen. "If you run, you might make the American flight if they have available seats. Terminal A, Gate Nine."

We shouldered our bags and took off. When we arrived at the gate, the waiting area was empty, and the agents were closing the doors.

"We need to get on that flight," Tom burst out, breathless, as we raced up to the counter. "Are there any seats left?"

"Yeah, there are, but we can't sell tickets here. You need to go to the ticketing counter," the agent exchanged a questioning look with her co-worker.

"But you could call the airline direct," the second agent said, "and buy a ticket over the phone if you have a credit card."

"Got the number?" Tom whipped out his phone.

We purchased tickets in less than ten minutes and boarded the plane, scheduled to arrive in Minnesota just after 11:00 p.m.

Confined in an aircraft, time seemed to disappear. I cycled through disbelief that Michael was dead and remorse at lost opportunities, and all the while, Tom rode the roller-coaster of emotions with me.

We made the trip from Skagway to Minnesota in less than twelve hours—record time.

As we descended into Minneapolis/St. Paul, I finally noted the scene outside the window. The metropolitan area spread out below us, thousands of blinking lights in every direction, when suddenly fireworks bloomed as if on cue at regular intervals in the surrounding night sky. Bright blazes of color in short bursts of intensity flared and faded in a fitting parallel to Michael's brief time on Earth, cascading down to wither from view, fizzling out in streamers.

My brother's craftsman-style house loomed dark at the end of the cul-de-sac, the porch lit dimly as we pulled up. The expansive lawn disappeared into the darkness, the sliver of waning crescent moon too little to illuminate. The humid air carried remnants of dinnertime grilling.

Miles, Bobby, and Maggie met us at the door.

"Oh, Cand, I'm so sorry," Miles pulled me in for a bear hug, followed by Maggie's less enveloping embrace and Bobby's stiff and quick stand-offish squeeze. They tripped over each other trying to grab our bags, the awkwardness thick as the damp air.

They'd never met Michael, and until our recent reunion, had rarely referred to him. But despite not knowing what to say or do, I appreciated their show of solidarity.

We deposited our bags in the spare bedroom, and then moved to the bar. Several empty beer bottles and an open bag of chips littered the countertop while 70s soft rock music filtered down from the in-ceiling speakers.

"Thanks for letting us crash here. And sorry for keeping you up so late," Tom accepted a glass of water. "We're gonna try to get a little sleep and take off sometime late morning. We don't really know how things will play out, but we're scheduled to fly home Monday. We may or may not make it back here after the funeral; hope you're okay with being flexible."

"No problem, whatever you guys need. You're welcome anytime," Miles said. Tom and I enjoyed at least one long weekend with my brother's family each winter we spent in Minnesota. "I don't think I'm going to go to the funeral, though. I've got a doctor's appointment tomorrow."

"Yeah, me neither, sis," Bobby said.

Maggie planned to come on Saturday and connect with Steph to see if they could drive together.

"Mom plans to drive herself tomorrow afternoon," Maggie said offhandedly.

I bristled. "I don't want Mom there."

All three siblings turned to me as one and stared. None of them knew how mom had reacted when I'd placed Michael for adoption or why our relationship was so strained.

"Cand, you can't do that," Maggie finally said. "He's her grandchild."

Heat flooded my whole body, and saliva pooled in my mouth. Tom came up and put an arm around me but didn't say anything. I licked my lips, opened my mouth, then closed it and shook my head. I didn't have the strength or even know how to explain, so I just turned and went to bed.

CHAPTER 22

The Following Morning—July 5, 2013
Would Have Been 23 Years Old

After a few hours of sleep, a shower, and some strong coffee, Tom and I drove the two-and-a-half hours to Marshall. During the drive, nausea took hold.

What if David decides he doesn't want me there?

I broke out in a cold sweat, and I could feel my heart thudding in my chest.

I don't belong here. I gave him away. I don't deserve to be here.

By the time we arrived, I'd worked myself into a panic. I'd convinced myself David would say that we shouldn't have come. I expected rejection at every turn. By David. By John, Michael's older brother. By all of Michael's family and friends. I was an outsider. I was sure everyone would see me as the woman who had abandoned her child.

Our one face-to-face get-together had included only Michael and David, and the prospect of meeting his entire extended family terrified me. It loomed like a monster in the closet, but there was absolutely no way I was going to miss my opportunity to see Michael one last time.

As we pulled onto the residential street, I tried to shift my focus away from the internal dialogue and rising panic. I noted the sprawling homes with their manicured lawns and American flags, so different from the winter starkness of our previous visit. Bright, rainbow-colored perennial beds and blooming rose bushes sprinkled the neighborhood as if they'd been painted in oil. At the same time, statuesque trees and shrubs trimmed neatly into spheres or cubes added orderliness and affluence.

Then, Michael's house.

We parked again along the cul-de-sac.

A lawnmower hummed somewhere down the street.

As Tom and I strode up to the house, the door swung wide. David stepped out, and without hesitation, engulfed me in a huge hug. Tears leaked from the corners of his eyes, and he clung to me, and I to him. At that moment, the truth came slamming home: He was my remaining connection to Michael. David possessed all the memories, history, and details that made Michael who he was, and I tightened my grip.

"Candace, this is Lori," David stepped aside to make room on the porch for a petite woman with short, sandy blond hair.

"Oh, I'm so glad you made it." She smelled of lilacs and soap, and when she folded me in her arms, her embrace carried the warmth of coming home. "Please, come inside." We slipped off our shoes and followed her into the living room. "We're still collecting things to bring to the funeral home," she said, pointing to the formal dining room where a group of blond-haired girls and women hovered over a table.

Warm oak trim and gilded frames caught the early afternoon light streaming in through the windows. Bulky, brown leather furniture stood against cream carpet so soft and plush that my stocking feet sunk into the pile. A cluster of cushions sat below a large bay window where I imagined Michael had read or played games on his phone. I didn't remember much of the inside of the house from our last visit – too distracted by Michael – but now I could envision how this house had provided my son what I could not, and my inner voice, ever vigilant and critical, seesawed between relief and jealousy.

"Hey girls, this is Michael's mom, Candace," Lori said.

I reeled back as if struck – *Michael's mom!*

Lori stepped aside casually as everyone at the table, each a version of Lori, got up to share a hug. We exchanged names and muted condolences, which I regret to say have blurred with sadness and time.

David led us to a spare bedroom, where Tom and I changed into appropriate attire. Dressed conservatively, I in a white sleeveless blouse with front ruffles and a slim fitted black skirt and Tom in black dress slacks and a short-sleeve button-up, we came back out to the dining room.

The farm-house style table and chairs sat bordered on one side by a large fireplace and the other with floor-to-ceiling windows. I remembered the windows from last time but not the fireplace. Lori got us each a glass of water, and offered us a snack, which we declined, then went to dress for the Wake too.

Tom and I carried flowers, pictures, and mementos from the house to a minivan, along with everyone else, in solemn silence, and then we rode with Lori and David to the funeral home, just the four of us. I stared at the fragments of Michael's life with a mixture of longing and disconnection, the memories scattered around like flower petals. Framed photos of Michael at various ages, stacked vertically in a clear tote, so I could just see edges of his hair or the color of his shirt, but not the whole image. A white poster board, one of several, where snapshots from Michael's life had been taped at random angles like a grade school art project, beautifully capturing his love-filled life. His contact juggling crystal ball and Scrappy, Michael's favorite stuffed animal as a child. While I wished I could see myself in these scattered memories, I chastised myself for such thoughts.

Once we'd brought everything into the foyer, David took me by the elbow, and we walked together into the main hall. Chairs arranged in rows faced the casket, prominently placed at the intersection of a large "L." Surrounding the casket were tables and easels filled to bursting with white flowers in pale vases with silver ribbons as if colorlessness could lighten the mood.

Tom took my other arm, and the three of us walked to the open casket. Tears streamed down my cheeks as I gazed upon my son for the second time since his adoption.

I do not know how long we stood like that, the three of us arm-in-arm, but eventually, I found myself alone. Michael lay in peaceful repose. The attempt to recreate his youthful glow with makeup merely highlighted his lifelessness. This was just a shell; he was already gone. I ran my fingers along the buttons of his dress shirt, repulsed by the stiffness beneath, yet wanting one last chance at physical contact.

"I'm sorry," I said. "I'm sorry I didn't try harder," each word becoming more strained, "I'm sorry we didn't have more time. I'm sorry I couldn't be your mom." I hung my head, tears dripping as I gripped the edge of the coffin, and my body shook with silent sobs.

Throughout the Wake, the more informal gathering before the funeral the following day, people sifted in and out of the room and approached me, asking, "Are you Mike's mom?" to which I could only nod my head. David, Lori, and John introduced me to so many of Michael's family and friends, all of whom paid their respects to me as his mother. I didn't know how to accept the compassion and recognition, let alone the attention. I felt honored and unworthy, a horrible dichotomy.

I relived my decision to place him for adoption throughout the hours-long wake, replayed our only meeting, and cowered under crushing regret. All the while, Tom kept pace with my erratic emotions; he sat with me when I needed stillness, moved me when I needed to break the destructive cyclic internal dialogue, and cushioned the overwhelming number of people who wanted to meet me. And I cried. I cried like I hadn't cried since those days on Helen's couch after I'd signed away my parental rights. Raw, grotesque, snot-filled weeping. But unlike twenty-three years earlier, I couldn't stop it. I couldn't hold it in and wait for solitude or privacy. My ability to shut it out, numb myself, and dissociate failed me. This was a tidal wave, a category four hurricane, an EF5 tornado, and I was helpless against it.

At some point, days later, Tom wondered aloud how anyone could cry so much; he had never experienced such retching sadness.

I had.

And there was no running from this tsunami.

CHAPTER 23

Evening—July 5, 2013

The quiet neighborhood, which earlier had flaunted vivid flowers and crisp edges, slumbered in the falling daylight as if the brushstrokes had shifted from oil to watercolor. More than a dozen vehicles lined the street leading up to the house, and as I slipped out of the rental car, the air appeared brighter, even though dusk approached.

My eyes, face, and whole body felt puffy, but I was not tired despite the four emotionally charged hours at the funeral home.

Light streamed through slits in the curtained windows as we approached the front door. It was ajar, as if in welcome; laughter and boisterous conversation floated out to greet us. Tom rang the bell.

"Please, come inside," David took my hand. "Most of the family is already here."

Tom and I glanced at each other. My lips curved into the hint of a smile, honored by the welcome.

People filled the house—aunts and uncles, sisters, cousins, and friends, milling about with wine and beer in hand, speaking in small clusters, the whispered tones of the Wake left behind to make room for the time-honored tradition of the Irish Wake.

"How are you?" Tom whispered. "Are you in a good enough headspace to have a glass of wine?" Tom and I had a pact we'd made when we got married regarding drinking. Three rules: no drinking alone, no drinking and driving, and no drinking when upset.

"I think so." I dipped my head in thought. "Yes. I'm sad, for sure, but I don't feel the desolation I felt at the funeral home. I kinda feel lighter but grounded too. Does that make sense?"

"Totally. And everyone is so genuinely grateful we're here. It feels so... right." He put his arm around my shoulder.

I nodded and leaned into him. After getting us each a glass of merlot, we navigated the space together as a team. I surrendered to everone's desire to meet me and fully embraced my role as Michael's mother as best I could, in large part because of their warm welcome.

I lost track of how many times a conversation began with "You look just like Mike," or comments about the set of my eyes, the shape of my nose, my hair color, or skin tone. And, I think maybe because of that resemblance, they instinctively extended their acceptance.

Tom and I shared some of our stories, how we met, and where we lived, relieved to shrug off the cloak of grief, even if just briefly.

And time and time again, I heard these words: "Thank you. Thank you for giving Michael to us, for sharing him with us."

After hours of talking, laughter, and toasts to Michael, I leaned back in the car's passenger seat and closed my eyes. Warmth spread through my body, covering me like a blanket as my heart surged with love and grief for Michael's family. These strangers, who seemed to regard me as family, shared my loss. I felt assured in the knowledge that what I'd just experienced was the same thing Michael had grown up with, and consequently, I knew that I had chosen correctly so many years before.

We had arranged to share a hotel room with my sister, Stacy, who was still enroute by car from south of St. Louis. Exhausted, Tom and I went straight to bed. I'm not even sure if I brushed my teeth, and I didn't hear her arrive.

Stacy and I shared a history of trauma and a contentious relationship with our mother. We talked on the phone every three or four months, but I hadn't seen her in well over a year. Two years my senior, she had openly referred to Michael as her nephew and had expressed hopes of one day meeting him.

In the morning, I opened my eyes to see Stacy staring back at me from the other bed, head on her pillow just like mine.

"Hey," her eyes glistened with unshed tears.

"Hey." My tears immediately slipped over the bridge of my nose to fall on the pillowcase. "I'm so glad you came," I choked but made no move to get up yet.

Stacy bore witness to my sorrow from the other bed for a while, and when I got up, we embraced. Our bodies trembled in unison, her sobs echoing mine, as we left wet patches on our pajama tops and slime in our hair.

Tom had learned that Michael's friends planned to pay tribute to his love of Dr. Who by wearing bow ties to the funeral, so while we got ready, he went off in search of his own bow tie and a plaid shirt. Stacy and I shared the mirror, makeup, and the blow dryer, just like when we were teenagers. The familiarity and camaraderie provided a level of comfort I couldn't have received from anyone else.

Just before 10:00 a.m., we arrived at St. Stephen Lutheran Church, a sprawling single-story brick building capped on one side with a steep-peaked roof culminating at a three-story bell tower. Bright green grass, sparkling with dew, spread out for acres around the church and parking lot.

We found David in the antechamber, and after sharing a long embrace, he held me at arms-length and said, "We'd like you and your whole family to sit with us during the ceremony."

Heat rushed to my cheeks, and I couldn't speak. The invitation was an honor, but I didn't know what to say. I didn't feel worthy and knew Mom was coming. I looked at Tom and silently pleaded with him to help, which he seemed to understand immediately.

"Candace has a complex relationship with her mom," Tom said, letting his words trail away as I propped up against him.

David acknowledged my discomfort with a slow nod and reached for my hand, squeezing it. "Michael is over there in the vestibule if you'd like to see him. I've got to talk to our priest, but I'm so grateful you are here. We all are." Tears stood out in his eyes. He turned to Tom, "You too."

The church lobby opened into a spacious gallery with flaxen walls and taupe carpet brightly lit by recessed can lights. Michael's ivory casket sat open at the back of the room, tucked tightly against the wall.

I lingered at the edge of the casket, noting his crisp button-up shirt, colorful bow tie, and black, thick-rimmed glasses—a big boy-man with soft features and broad shoulders. I don't know how long I stood there, trying to memorize his features, but when Tom came to lead me away, I was surprised by scores of people shuffling through the vestibule, grown loud with murmurs and whispers. Tom tucked me into a corner, where I watched them, singly and in pairs, gaze down at Michael, lips moving in silent conversation, and I smiled as one of his friends slipped a joint into his breast pocket.

Maggie and Steph, with Stacy and Mom, shuffled over to where Michael lay. I instinctively tensed when I saw Mom and hid behind Tom, peeking over his shoulder to glare at her.

How dare she come! She didn't deserve to be here. "He's dead to me," replayed in my memory.

Now, he really was dead.

I felt nauseous as years of pent-up emotion churned in my gut—a toxic mixture of abandonment and anger, loneliness, and misunderstanding. I thought my head would explode, or I was going to throw up, or both.

"Would you go get Stacy for me?" I asked Tom. He slipped away, leaving me in my defensible corner.

Stacy's blond, shoulder-length waves bobbed above her black, square-neck pencil dress as she crossed the room. I looked down. Tom had chosen an almost identical dress for me, and I was grateful. At least I could *look* good.

"I don't want to talk to her," the words spewed from my mouth like spit. "I don't want her near me." All my hoarded rage came out in a fury.

"Well, I'll do what I can," Stacy said, unfazed by my anger. "But you know how she is. I'll let Maggie and Steph know, too; see if they can help."

Less than ten minutes later, from across the room, I heard Mom's voice above the din as she proclaimed, "He's my grandson." The sound jabbed twin burning needles into my temples. I turned and glared. Stacy looked over to me, resignation in her stare and something else, almost like she was trapped, unable to rein Mom in. She half shrugged her shoulders as I escaped outside.

Throughout the morning viewing, anytime I was in the vestibule, I could hear Mom's voice, taking credit for being his grandma, claiming a pride that just made me seethe. *How dare she!* When they closed the casket and moved him into the church proper, I sought out Stacy again.

"I can't stop her," Stacy said. She was flushed and looking furtively around. "She's just so... *Mom!*"

"I know. But please, keep her with you for the service. Please? We're gonna sit behind Michael's family," I pointed to the right-center section, "So, can you take her somewhere else?"

"I'll take her to sit with me, Maggie, and Steph. We should be able to keep her there." She paused. "I'd never seen him before," she whispered. Then she lightly touched my face, "He's so beautiful, Cand. He looks just like you."

My expression melted under her touch, and I gasped. Her words hit like a slap in the face, so kind yet so painful.

Tom and I held hands as we entered the nave. It was gigantic. It had room for at least four hundred people, and it was filling up. Wide aisles separated the wood pews into four sections, fanning out from the dais. The ceiling rose sharply from the entryway ending above the altar. White walls and tall, clear windows added to the spaciousness. Sounds resonated through the room, making it seem like my ears had water in them.

As we slipped into a pew about a dozen rows behind the family, a hush slowly fell, and everyone took their places. Tissues captured sniffles, and sobs were swallowed. Suddenly, a woman's cries rose in waves behind me. Immediately I felt tethered to her, and every time her wails rose, they tugged me along with her, tears and empathy out of my control. I would later discover that she'd had a close relationship with Michael; she was Hannah's aunt.

When the ceremony was complete, the pallbearers carried him out, followed by the rest of us. Lori approached Tom and me as we made our way to the parking lot.

"We'd like you to follow right behind us for the drive out to the cemetery, okay?"

"Thank you, Lori, that means a lot," Tom replied.

"You're his mother," she reached for both my hands, "You should be up with us."

I couldn't speak. A lump lodged in my throat.

Slumped in the passenger seat, I gazed into the side mirror at the cars that snaked for what seemed like miles behind us. Their haloed headlights proclaiming Michael's last march.

We drove for what seemed a long time until we came to the small graveyard, which abutted a county road. I stepped out of the car to a rush of strangeness, an almost out-of-body experience. All around, people walked in slow motion through the manicured green grass, angling toward the casket being pulled from the hearse. Women in high heels stepped carefully, trying not to sink into the earth, while men held their elbows, looking uncertain yet determined.

As we wove between headstones, I noticed recurrent surnames clustered together. Some stones were big, some small, but all were made from shiny black granite as if the darkness of the material would ease the sight of seeing your loved one's name etched forever in stone.

David smiled sadly and gestured next to him and John. I came toward him but wondered how I fit here. I didn't even know Michael, yet this group of people honored me with a front-row seat. And even though my mind continued to scream I was unworthy - I'd abandoned him and didn't belong here - I felt such warmth standing beside them.

When the graveside service was complete, David walked to a neighboring gravestone, stopped, and placed his hands on it. Bowing his head, tears glistened in the sunlight as they dropped to the ground, one after the other. It was Jane's gravestone.

I gaped in shock at the date, July 2. Jane had died one day and thirteen years before Michael.

Oh my goddess! My heart lurched, fighting to claw its way out of my chest. *They died one day apart!* I turned away, horror-stricken, not wanting to see the crushing pain on his face. I couldn't fathom how he was capable of functioning. My grief was forgotten, if only for a moment, and all I could think about was the crushing anguish David and John must be experiencing.

I'd had no idea.

Although I knew of Jane's death, I'd never questioned anyone about her passing, and I had no idea of the actual date.

Fighting to breathe, I stumbled away from the gaping hole.

All the young adults, Michael and John's friends, had gathered on the grass on the other side of the parked cars. They stood casually in a row, heads bent together, talking in twos and threes. All wore bow ties, boys and girls both, some in jeans and t-shirts, some in dresses and slacks.

John broke away from the pack, walking towards Tom and me,

followed by a young man with a goatee and wire-rimmed glasses.

"Hi, this is Josh, one of Michael's best friends," John said. "Josh, this is Candace, Michael's birth mom."

"It's so nice to meet you."

"You too," I tried to smile.

"Michael saved my life," Josh paused for just a second. "A few years ago, I was horribly depressed and was going to commit suicide. He talked me down and convinced me to live. I thought you should know. If it weren't for you giving him away, I wouldn't be here today. And I just wanted to say thank you."

My heart, bruised and battered by Michael's death and pierced with the new knowledge regarding Jane's passing, found a semblance of respite with this knowledge of Michael's compassion. And something else: Even though there was no indication he'd taken his own life, there was still a tiny part of me that worried. If Michael had talked a friend down from the edge, it had to mean he couldn't have committed suicide.

CHAPTER 24

The Next Day July 7, 2013

My reflection in the small, oval airplane window revealed dark circles under my eyes and accusation. *Why hadn't I talked about Michael more?* Regret had been festering in my gut since I woke. It roiled and mounted with every mile we traveled toward home—a gnawing mix of deep disappointment, fruitless longing, and unavailing remorse. I scowled at the woman in the glass and decided. *I'm not going to hide him anymore.*

"I want to have a remembrance ceremony in Skagway. I need people to know about Michael. I want to share how important he was." My declaration, strong to start, ended in a whimper and a collapse into tears.

Tom pulled me into his embrace. Patient as ever, he waited for the wave to subside.

"Okay, what are you thinking?"

"Well, I think I want to do it soon, maybe in the next few days?" He nodded.

"I want to eulogize him, but I also want to share my story. The adoption, our reunion, everything." As soon as I said it aloud, I knew this was exactly what I needed to do.

Tom steered the conversation that followed, asking questions to keep me focused and narrow down the event's details. It would be open to the whole community, but I didn't want a service, just a gathering, a chance to share Michael.

"I'll take care of logistics, and I think you should work on what you want to say. Why don't you use the notes app on your phone and get started now?"

Preparing for the gathering provided a focus for my grief, both easing and honoring what I was experiencing. Once home, I sat on the couch, writing and crying in equal measure, a cathartic and exhausting undertaking.

On the day of the memorial, the Elks Lodge meeting room with its low ceilings and dark furniture seemed to project and reflect melancholy. Hickory brown loveseats and matching chairs sat along the room's perimeter, and rows of black, stackable chairs marched in rows down the center. A bouquet of local flowers sat atop a four-by-four-foot podium, and off to the side, a large-screen TV played Michael's funeral video. David had given me the film along with Scrappy, Michael's favorite stuffed animal from childhood. With matted tan fur, the toy dog sat in the center of a folding table surrounded by framed pictures of Michael.

Tom and I stood near the podium, watching as people slowly arrived and accepting condolences and hugs from our friends and closest acquaintances. Clusters of folks murmured while the chairs filled. There were far more people than I'd expected, and tears of gratitude mingled with those of grief.

"How are you doing?" Tom's expression clouded. It was ten minutes past the scheduled start. "Can you go through with it?"

I had shared with him my fear of reading aloud what I'd written, but also my belief that the only way I would reap actual benefits was if I did it myself.

"I can read it for you if you want, you know."

"No, I really need to do this. I'm ready." I gave him a swift nod and clasped my four-page speech in clammy hands.

"Okay, everyone. We're about to begin. Can you find a seat, please?" He turned back toward me, reaching for both my hands, his thumbs rubbing softly back and forth. Whispered conversations faded as the room quieted. He released me and faced the crowd.

"Thank you all so much for coming today. The passing of Candace's son, Michael, has been one of the most difficult things we have ever experienced. I know that many of you were surprised to learn that Candace had a son at all. She's very private about it but now hopes to share him with you. This gathering is a way for us to open our lives and hearts in hopes of finding healing. Candace?" He turned to me expectantly.

Taking a purposeful breath, I stepped forward. *I need to do this.* "Stay next to me?" I whispered.

He nodded.

I lifted the printed pages. I'd read through it a hundred times. But this was the time that counted.

"How do I begin? I guess by telling you I'm a woman who had a baby and gave him up for adoption." I stopped. Such a simple statement, but one I'd rarely uttered.

"A woman who was lucky enough to have had the chance to meet him as an adult and a little time to get to know him. A birthparent that was welcomed at the funeral, given a place of honor at the services, and offered sympathy by his loved ones and friends." I could feel my love for Michael's family holding me up.

"There were many times I was asked, 'Are you his mom?' and I said, 'Yes.'" I paused, reveling in that proclamation. "And I can't tell you how much that meant to me, both that I was asked and that I could say, 'Yes.'" I swallowed a sob.

I will do this, even if it takes me all day. I will.

"So sad it's taken me this long to get here." I took a tissue from the podium, wiped my eyes, then took a conscious breath and sent the air deep into my diaphragm.

"I want to open up about Michael. Ask for help. What I want you to know is that even though I placed Michael for adoption, he has always been a significant part of my life and a huge factor in who I am today." I sighed. "I need to share this because it feels like it's my last chance.

"Because I lost my son. Again." My chest caved in as a river of grief flowed from my eyes. Tom reached over, placed a hand on the small of my back, which grounded me and helped me regain my composure.

"The first time was by choice." The thickness of my voice filled the room. "I gave him up so he could have a better life. I gave him up because I believed I couldn't give him what he needed to grow and to thrive." Would they understand? They had to understand. *Please, understand.* "I gave him up by choice–but I can tell you it was the hardest thing I've ever done in my life. I grieved and grieved for him. And I grieved alone.

"I struggled with sharing my grief because this was what I had chosen. I *chose* to let him go. I *chose* to forgo being a parent." The words spit from my mouth like cherry pits. "I gave up my chance to kiss a scraped knee or soothe a sunburn, to hang kindergarten drawings on my fridge," a sob escaped. I swallowed. *Slow down.*

"Or go to school plays. I'd never have to ground him or take away his phone." A few chuckles came from those gathered. "And I thought that giving all of this up meant I couldn't ask for comfort in my grief, so I faced it alone." I repositioned, standing taller. *I will not face it alone, ever again.*

"What I need to tell you is that I never stopped looking for him in crowds, at malls, and walking down streets. I never stopped thinking about him." I paused, looking up at sympathetic faces, eyes glinting with unshed tears. "And I never stopped loving him." Another tissue caught the drips from my nose.

"And then, one day, five years ago, he contacted me. I hadn't planned for this call, but I'd always hoped for it." My voice grew in volume and strength as I tapped into the joy and beauty of reuniting with Michael. "We began emailing–sharing parts of our lives, testing the water." Tom had dropped his hand, and I saw a slight smile on his lips.

"They were infrequent communiqués with tidbits of our lives. We weren't in a hurry–there would be time. And I wanted our inter-actions to be on his terms, not mine. I needed him to have control over how our relationship progressed. Two years would pass until the day came when he asked if we could meet." I stopped to relish a warmth blooming in my chest. "As you can probably imagine, I was ecstatic!" I tilted my head back, eyes rolling to the sky. "To see his face, to hear his voice, share his laughter, give him a hug!" Dropping my head, I continued, "I cannot adequately express to you the excitement I felt as I prepared to meet him. And then, the pride and the sheer joy of holding him in my arms." I crossed my arms, speech in one hand while the other absently rubbed my upper arm. "We spent hours together. Tom and I with Michael and David, his adoptive dad. It was amazing and wonderful!" Around the room, smiles lit up faces.

"It would be the only time we saw each other face to face." *Forge on. I can't stop here.* "And I am so grateful!" My heart lifted, spurring me to continue.

"Since that day, we had made plans to meet again—a few times. Plans that always seemed to fall through, but we were taking it slowly. There would be time.

"So, Michael and I shared emails and texts, and I started opening up about him." I made eye contact with Julie, Kathy, and Jan, those friends who'd been privy to Michael. "I put a framed photo of us up in the house and posted it on Facebook. I started sharing some of my guarded optimism for the future—a future where I might be able to be a mom for Michael. Where birthday phone calls would be the norm and not something I had to agonize over. Do I do it, do I not? Do I call, or do I text? What should I say? How do I make sure I don't scare him away? On and on. I was so excited about the possibilities of the future, yet so afraid I'd screw it up! Take it slow, I kept reminding myself. Take it slow and build a foundation.

"We had time." The words on the page blurred. I stopped, dabbed my eyes, and took another deep breath. I never imagined we wouldn't.

"In early 2012, he 'friended' us on Facebook–you have no idea how excited we were! Such a fantastic window into his life! I felt pride in the man he was becoming and excited for what the future would bring. A few months ago, Tom and I started talking about inviting him to Skagway. Give him a chance to try something new–spread his wings and fly. And, if that gave us more opportunity to build our relationship with him–all the better! We were waiting for the right time to bring it up." My throat tightened. "There was no pressure," tears formed. "We had time." Desperation forced my voice into a high pitch. "His life was just beginning; he'd just turned 23."

I can't. Oh, my Goddess! I can't. Yes, yes, you can.

It felt like forever before I regained my voice. *Breathe.* Softly, I went on, "The last time I heard from Michael was on Mother's Day. He sent me this text: 'Happy Mother's Day. Thank you for making such a hard choice, so I had the chance at a better life.'" The thickness in my throat threatened to choke me, and I struggled to push through.

I stood before my community, feeling naked and raw. But I finally knew that I had every right to grieve, that the world could bear to hear it now, and that the vulnerability wouldn't destroy me. I stood taller and planted my feet firmly on the floor, made eye contact with several people, and dared them to say otherwise. Courage surged in my veins.

"I lost my son. Again." I hiccupped. "This time, he slipped away, and it wasn't by choice, and he won't be coming back. And I grieve." My words started coming clipped and guttural. "I grieve for a future that's been lost. And today, I'll grieve like any mother who didn't have enough time with her son."

It seemed as though the room erupted in sorrow around me: whimpers, sniffles, noses being blown, but perhaps it was just my sadness, unleashed.

Tom reached over again, put his arm around me, and smiled sadly as he tucked my head into his shoulder. I leaned briefly, wiped my face, then took another slow, deep breath. I turned back to the assembly.

"Michael was loved very deeply. He had a huge family that spent a lot of time together and many close friends. David, his adopted dad, was so warm and open-hearted to us both, inviting us to be with him and the whole family at their home and during the services." My voice took on a lilting quality. "Michael's brother, John, who's also adopted, went out of his way to bring Michael's friends over to introduce them to us. Michael's stepmother, Lori, and his Aunt Linda were always there to ensure we knew where to sit whenever we looked like we didn't know what to do or where to go. Hugs were many, and often. Michael was very close to many of his nieces, and some of the fiercest hugs and cutest stories were from them." I smiled in remembrance.

"Many of Michael's friends knew who we were." I smiled broadly at the whole room. "One told me about when Michael was getting ready to 'friend' us on Facebook. There were about ten of them lounging together when Michael finally sent the friend request–he was excited too." Inwardly, I appreciated how this small detail could inspire so much joy.

"There were many who said thank you. Thank you for sharing Michael, for letting him be a part of their family. Thank you for coming from so far away so that we could meet you.

"And I had the chance to say thank you, too. For giving him a wonderful home filled with love." My voice hitched. "For supporting him and taking care of him. For helping him to become the wonderful young man he was."

I turned to the last page. Although I stood erect, I felt drained. I nodded to Tom. *Almost done.*

"And now, I say thank you to all of you. For coming here today and giving me this opportunity to share with you a big part of who I am, for giving me support and comfort.

"And especially, I say thank you to Tom. Who encouraged me to pursue an open relationship with Michael, who shared my hopes and dreams for our future." I turned partially to face him and set the printed pages on the podium. "Who grieves for my loss and recognizes it as his own. Who has held my hand, wiped my tears, and guided me through this process with gentle strength and kindness. Thank you for helping me say goodbye."

His arms rose as I walked into his embrace. A sense of lightness suffused my being. I inhaled; Tom's masculine scent comforted my bruised soul. We remained entwined briefly, then he shifted, holding me at arm's length, making eye contact.

"My turn," he whispered, smiling wanly, then released me, pulling the prepared speech from his suit coat pocket. He scanned the room, then began.

"I will begin by telling you I'm a man who has not fathered a child.

"I have known Candace since we were teenagers. I knew her when she was pregnant with Michael, and I knew she had given him up. When we started dating, I came to find out how deeply she cared for the son she had placed for adoption. How she struggled to express her feelings, how she struggled with her sense of motherhood."

I shifted close behind Tom. I took comfort in looking at his distinctive profile, hair pulled back in a ponytail, and his distinctive ducktail beard.

"I would ask every Mother's Day if she would want to have a quiet celebration, a card, or flowers… Often it would be a dinner by ourselves. The time around Michael's birthday was often difficult, and Candace would usually commemorate it by herself. I tried to be there for her…

"And then all that began to change…

"When the day came that Michael reached out to her…

"What a sense of relief, hope, exuberance! … and fear.

"Relief…no longer would she wonder if he was okay.

"Hope….to begin a relationship with him.

"Exuberance…that he wanted to know about her."

"And fear…that he might be angry with her, that she would scare him away, that he wouldn't like her."

I marveled at how well he knew me and how close we'd been during this ordeal; how he always seemed to know what I was thinking and feeling, especially during the Wake and funeral.

"Michael did want to know about her," his voice lifted, amplifying his words. "He was okay; he was happy. Hope was the present emotion…so much hope, and time, we had time." He paused, brows furrowed, then seemed to shake off whatever it was.

"Slowly, we communicated, began to learn about one another. Then meeting face to face with Michael, seeing in his eyes the happiness, understanding, curiosity, admiration. Truly knowing he wasn't mad with her, that this relationship would continue and grow." He raised his head, turning to me, eyes moist with tears. When he turned away, though, his eyes were clear.

"I was there for this meeting…and as I looked at him, a thought had come to the surface. I know it was already there, probably the day Michael reached out to Candace…" He shook his head, almost like he was trying to dispel the thought, "and it was this: I had made my decision not to have a planned child, and I was at peace with it…but this boy, this child was of Candace … I would want nothing more… than to nurture this relationship, and someday…maybe he would consider me as another father figure in his life."

My heart would've burst if it weren't already broken.

"I would have a chance to experience fatherhood, maybe to be a grandfather.

"So, Candace and I began to dream, to let ourselves dream…" He'd reached blindly behind him with one hand, and when I grabbed it, he turned and lifted his face. No smile nor tears were visible, but I could still see the lingering remnants of hope.

"Candace was also more willing to let our friends know of this very special relationship. To no longer be silent with her feelings about Michael. To take pride in him, herself, and their newfound relationship.

"Michael left us too soon; we had so many hopes and dreams, but I take solace in what he gave back to Candace, what he gave me… when he reached out, he gave Candace back hope, a real hope, an attainable hope…and we cherished it. It may have been too short, but it was real, and it was beautiful." Now when he turned to look at me, a genuine smile spread across his face.

"I had always believed everyone here would come to know this about Michael and that our relationship would be commonly known. That you would meet Michael with Candace and I, grinning proudly at his side. This I tell you, so that you may understand. This is our chance to tell you about Michael." His pace slowed, and he drew out each remaining word, "That we were proud of him and that we loved him." My body now gently shook as I fought to keep any sound from escaping.

Taking a breath, then sighing as he scanned the room again, he finished, "I am grateful for the love and support we find here. That you have come to listen, to console, to support us. Thank you."

CHAPTER 25

Later That Week—July 12

M aroon carpet and wood paneling absorbed what little light seeped into the living room under the blinds. A water bottle, coffee mug, and box of tissues crowded the corner of the end table, and Luna slept in my lap. I hadn't opened the shades, showered, or left the house, not even to walk Luna, since the memorial three days prior.

"Are you gonna be okay?" Concern etched Tom's face.

"Yeah," I sighed.

"You sure? I can stay home if you want." He waited, and then walked over and kissed me on the forehead. "All right. Just call me if you need anything. I'm a block away. I love you." As he stood up, he added, "You *are* gonna be okay."

I wasn't so sure. I thought I'd taken a giant step forward at the memorial—sharing my vulnerability and pain—only to feel stuck again. I sat hour after hour in my tattered robe, staring blindly at the floor or scrolling through Michael's Facebook page. Friends and loved ones posted memories, favorite songs, and condolences, and I read every new entry, jealousy and regret vying for dominance. Luna looked up expectantly whenever I shifted, then heavily lay her head back down, realizing I wasn't getting up.

When Tom returned from work, he packed for our annual excursion to The Atlin Music Festival to celebrate my birthday. We'd discussed the possibility of canceling, but we both knew that if there were anything that could cheer me up, it was music. Besides, did I want to spend my birthday holed up alone in the house?

The following week I tried to go to work.

"You don't need to be here," concern knit Julie's brows together. She strode briskly up to me, hugged me, then said, "You wanna try, though, don't you?"

She knew me so well. "Maybe it'll be a distraction?" I'd been calling her almost every day, just to check-in. She continued to insist I take as much time as I needed.

"All right," she said, "but just go when you need to, okay?"

I nodded.

I lasted less than ten minutes.

Toward the end of July, Julie agreed to try half days. We'd play it by ear and assess as we went along. She asserted that if I needed to leave for any reason, I only had to give her a look or a nod; no explanation required.

Tom stopped by the gallery daily, usually with chocolate. The times I felt particularly fragile, I'd shoot him a text with a single word: *help*. He'd call Julie during the short walk over so that when he arrived, he could sweep me out the back door.

As the director of a retail art gallery, I was responsible for managing both the sales floor and a staff of fifteen, but I proved woefully inept to do either in my current state of mind. I couldn't concentrate or problem-solve and often turned supervision over to Julie. As I grew stronger, I could at least operate as a salesperson. I'd worked in the business long enough to put myself on autopilot, extolling the virtues of one piece of art or painting while completely dissociating from myself.

But working in the public sphere offered other difficulties.

A blond boy, maybe twelve years old, stood with his back to me, chatting animatedly with his mother. His button-down dress shirt pooched out slightly at the waist, and his hands moved excitedly. He reminded me of a picture of Michael from fourth grade David had given me after the funeral. Suddenly, the boy turned, and I saw he had on a bright red bow tie. Not a clip-on, the real deal, just like Michael wore. And sky-blue eyes. His presence triggered a sense of loss so profound a sob escaped before I could leave the sales floor.

Boys who looked like Michael, at any age, made me do a double-take and then tear up, as did any teenager wearing a nose ring or ear plugs. Once, a woman standing a few feet away called out to her child in the back of the store, "Hey, Michael, come here," causing a hitch in my heart.

Panic attacks sent me rushing to the bathroom with heart palpitations, sweaty palms, and internal claustrophobia. I'd ball my hands and squeeze my eyes shut, keening into the void through gritted teeth, fighting for control. It felt eerily like after I'd signed away my parental rights.

But this time, unlike after the adoption, there was no stigma attached to my grief. There's nothing shameful about losing a child, right? But, people don't want to talk to a mother about her dead child. And most people automatically deflect with either questions or sanctimonious comments like "He's in a better place" and "God called him home," which made me seethe with anger.

Some questions were safe, like "When did he pass?" or "How old was he?" But those questions often led to one specific, unsafe question, "What was he like?" I didn't feel capable of answering that question. I hardly knew him. How could I explain missing something I never had?

And this cyclic mind trap triggered, like clockwork, the old negative tapes. Only this time, it was like a punch in the gut. "You weren't really his mother. You have no right to grieve."

So, rather than put myself in a position to have to feel or deflect, I said nothing. I didn't give people a chance, just like after the adoption. It was easier to block than to explain. Even though I declared my desire to share my pain at his memorial and not go it alone, I'd never learned *how* and seemed incapable of starting now.

Instead, Tom would find me, sitting on the recliner in the dark, Pink Floyd blaring on the stereo:

Now I've got that feeling once again
I can't explain, you would not understand
This is not how I am
I... have become comfortably numb...

Then, one day, I thought maybe there was one person who would completely understand, someone who's also grieving the loss of his son.

"I drafted an email to David," I said to Tom after dinner one evening in late July. I was working some but still felt numb, lost, and empty. "Last night, I read through what I'd written for Michael's memorial and realized I want to share it with David. I want him to know how grateful I am and how welcomed we felt at the funeral. And, well, I want to let him know I'm thinking about him and the whole family."

"That's really nice."

"And, I guess I'm kind of hoping he's interested in staying in contact. I just, I don't know, feel so alone." Tom's face clouded, and I quickly added, "You've been amazing, but I just feel like I'm missing something. Maybe connecting with David will help... I gotta *do* something. This is something." My shoulders raised in a what-have-I-got-to-lose vibe.

"Can I take a look?" He asked, reaching for the laptop. I willingly handed it over, our correspondence routine well-practiced.

"I'll take Luna for a walk, and when I get back, we can go over it together, okay?"

About half an hour later, I sat down next to Tom on the couch. "Well?"

"It's good. Really good. I think you expressed your gratitude well, our gratitude." He smiled. "Are you going to attach your whole speech?"

I nodded.

"You can send mine too. And, I'm glad you told him about our plans to invite Michael up here before he died."

"Yeah, I don't think we told David about that, right?"

"No, we didn't. I'm also happy you let him know we're open to staying in touch. I hope they do decide to take a trip to Alaska and look us up."

Ten days later, David replied.

Candace,
Thank you for a beautiful letter and sharing your feelings about your gathering.

I sighed in relief.

This was really powerful and spiritual for Lori and me. I wanted to let you know how much your presence during this time meant to myself, Lori, John, and really to all of our family. John, I believe, was especially touched that you and Tom were with us.

I couldn't stop the tears from flowing.

I believe he was able to internalize his own hopes of knowing his birth mother after seeing how much you and Tom both loved Michael. Michael and John turned out to both be very caring and good people. I am so proud of both of my boys, and I know how blessed I am.

I am still really struggling with a heavy heart in our loss of Michael. Our communities have been very good to us, but it is so difficult seeing people for the first time and having them come to offer their love and support.

I envisioned David having to repeat over and over what happened, and my heart went out to him.

Words just cannot express the feelings of loss and sadness we have. Getting to know you and Tom has been a comfort to us in sharing the hopes and dreams we all had for Michael.

I nodded to myself and wiped my cheeks.

Your love and friendship have created a bond between our families. We are thankful for this gift through Michael.
Love, Dave, Lori, John and the Girls

David's appreciation and openness reaffirmed the connection I'd felt at the funeral, and to learn that he was struggling too brought me comfort. Then, just two days later, he wrote again.

In the chaotic aftermath of the funeral, he'd lost our address. He also requested addresses for my sisters, probably to send thank you cards. But what I zeroed in on were these words:

I think about both of you every day and how you are feeling through all of this. The loss that you guys feel and how you shared it with your friends in Alaska was really important for you both. I [spend so] much time weeping. Mostly when alone. I am sure it is the same for you as well.

Here was fellowship, and interconnectedness, a shared identity: We were Michael's parents. In this letter, David reinforced my sense of belonging and lifted me, bringing grace and serenity. And, I wanted more.

I wrote him back. And so did Tom, separately. David replied within the week.

I have wanted to reach out to see how you and Tom have been but did not want to be a pest and keep bringing things back to you that are so difficult.

That was permission enough for me.

Soon, David and I exchanged letters almost every week. Sometimes he'd write first, sometimes I would, but in either case, it was as if we'd been anxiously waiting for the other to write and responded immediately.

Our letters almost always started by sharing how lost we felt, the all-encompassing sadness, and our difficulties speaking about him in public; how our tears were always near the surface, making people uncomfortable. Then, we'd ramble on about our families and how we stayed busy, the mundane activities of daily life. And to close, gratitude and appreciation for Michael, who brought us together, and how connecting was easing our pain.

In the fall, as we prepared for our annual trip to Minnesota, I told David we planned to come to Marshall. I wanted to visit Michael's gravesite. I would never miss an opportunity to visit him again. I also asked if David and Lori, and John too, might be interested in getting together.

"Guess what?" I asked Tom when he got home from work that night, even before he'd removed his jacket.

"What?"

"David invited us to stay with him and Lori when we come to visit," I walked backward as he crossed into the kitchen behind me.

"Really? That's awesome."

"He said we should come for dinner, spend the night, and then visit the cemetery together. I feel really lucky."

"We are lucky. Write him back. Tell him yes."

"You know, I always looked forward to the possibility of seeing Michael during our Minnesota visits, so I guess in a way, David and Lori will take his place."

But when the day came, despite the anticipation of seeing them, I experienced the same misgivings, uncertainty, and fear I felt during the drive to Marshall the first time and before the funeral. My concerns that Michael would change his mind, not like me, or be angry transferred to David and Lori.

"Why are you so worried?" Tom asked.

"I don't know." And I didn't. I couldn't explain my apprehension.

As we walked up to the house, there David stood, just like the last two times we'd been here. This time, a hopeful smile accompanied his tears. Without skipping a beat, he stepped forward to embrace me in a bear hug.

All my anxiety vanished.

Lori looked up from dinner preparations as we entered the kitchen, dropped what she was doing, and walked toward us, wiping her hands on her apron. "Oh, it's so wonderful to see you both. I'm so glad you came." Her easy, conversational tone and full embrace felt like coming home. And again, she smelled like lilacs and soap.

"How about a glass of wine?" David asked, reaching up to select a bottle from the built-in wine rack.

The warm light from the kitchen cast our shadows around the spacious room as Tom and I sat on stools at the center island. The last time we'd been there was after Michael's Wake when there were dozens of people and a cacophony of voices. The space now was quiet, cozy, and intimate.

"This was one of Michael's favorites," David handed me a bottle, his glassy tears catching the light. On the label, a carnival scene, colorful and merry, was topped with the banner, "Freakshow" Cabernet Sauvignon. I couldn't help but smile.

"Perfect."

"We finally heard from the medical examiner. Well, the second one."

Tom and I both stiffened. The first autopsy hadn't shown a reason for his death. I inclined my head to David.

"Natural causes," he said. "The only drug they found in his system was marijuana, and that was minimal. Nothing else," his eyes, which seemed constantly tear-filled, had cleared.

A barely audible sound, like the swish of a bird's wing, escaped my mouth and my whole body relaxed. Despite everyone's reassurance that Michael had not been depressed or suicidal, I had been unable to quash those fears completely. My years of research into reunion had uncovered a staggering statistic: Adoptees are four times more likely to attempt suicide than non-adoptees. But now, the worry I'd carried around since July that perhaps he'd committed suicide finally dissipated.

We spent the rest of the evening eating and drinking, crying, and laughing. Mostly crying. David told stories about Michael; Lori added the details she could, having joined the family during his teenage years. After dinner, David and Tom poured glasses of scotch. Our conversation flowed easily as if we'd been friends for years.

David and I cried throughout the evening, tag-team style, triggering each other endlessly. As the clock neared midnight, we called it quits, exhaustion evident in our slumped shoulders and bagging eyes.

In the morning, we had a light breakfast then drove out to the cemetery together. David and I walked to Michael's grave, yet unmarked, and stopped in unison at the perimeter. David reached over, pulling me next to him, and circled my shoulders with his arm. Eventually, he walked away, around to Jane's headstone, just to the north of Michael's. Lori and Tom had stayed in the car, but now I heard dried leaves crunch underfoot at their approach. Tom wrapped an arm around me, just like David had, remaining quiet.

"Hey Michael," he finally said. "Last month, I hiked up to the Devil's Punchbowl, up above Skagway, and I thought about you the whole way. I wish I could have taken you there. I wish we would've had more time to get to know each other.

"Candace and I are watching *Dr. Who* together. Can you believe she'd never seen it? But I wish we could have done that together too.

"We didn't have enough time, and I'm sorry. But I am so grateful that you reached out to Candace when you did and that we had a chance to meet you and get to know you a little.

"Candace loved you deeply, and I did too."

My sinuses had begun to tingle with early warnings of tears at his mention of *Dr. Who*, and by the time Tom finished, I was full-on weeping.

We stood together in silence. There was no need to hurry. A car sped by on the two-lane blacktop, the hum of the studded tires a signal that winter was around the corner.

"Do you want some alone time?" Tom asked.

I nodded, and he walked toward David, who was still standing by Jane's headstone. I wiped my nose with my coat sleeve.

"I wish we had more time, too," I whispered. "I wish I could have given you more. I wish…so many things." My tears had dried up, but my face felt hot and swollen. "And I'm so glad to get to know your dad." I looked up at David, my chest heavy with sadness for our shared loss but filled with newfound love. "I'm sorry I had to let you go as a baby, but I'm so happy I chose David." Fresh tears sprung, and at that moment, I recognized that even though I was crying, I didn't feel completely lost for the first time in a long time.

Back at the house, David led us to Michael's room, pointing out mementos, pictures, and knick-knacks. It smelled faintly musty, and I wondered when David had last visited but didn't ask.

He'd pick up an item, examine it briefly, then offer it to Tom or me. "You should have that."

By the time we left Michael's room, our arms were loaded with keepsakes. I couldn't wait to dive deep into the notebooks and other items but knew then was not the time.

Lori proudly took Tom to her sewing room after she discovered, to her delight, that Tom had won a blue ribbon at the state fair for one of his quilts. They stood head-to-head examining her brand-new long arm sewing machine and admiring her works-in-process.

"Wow, Tom, she has even more fabric than you!" I teased. We all laughed, knowing there was no way Tom would ever have as many fat quarters as Lori.

A few days later, back at our cabin, I wrote to David again.

Hi David,

Thank you so very much for opening your hearts and home to us. Again, as I prepare to leave Minnesota, I cannot adequately express my gratitude for all you have given Michael or all you've shared with us.

I feel reconnected and grounded again. I understand that for me, grief is cyclical, and all my feelings tend to ebb and flow. Sometimes I'm caught up in it, like being pulled under in an ocean's tide, flailing and fighting, which is how I've been feeling a lot lately. Other times I'm floating along with a river's current, still powerful and still not necessarily in "control," but at least not fighting everything around me.

Please give our love to the family and have a wonderful Thanksgiving. I know they say the holidays can be the hardest, but I will try to hug everyone tighter and be grateful for the family and love I have.

All our love,
Candace & Tom

CHAPTER 26

Two Months Later—December 2013
Would Have Been 23 Years Old

"I wish I knew what was going on in your head," Tom said. "I feel like our connection is gone, and I can't tell what you're thinking or feeling anymore. You seem so…lost."

"Yeah." I sighed. "I *feel* lost." The tether Tom and I had experienced when Michael died had broken, and I struggled to communicate my growing unease.

The emotional turmoil had returned and overshadowed the entire Yuletide Season. Usually, I loved December in Skagway. Instead, I was listless at Wednesday night holiday choir practices and didn't even go to the tree lighting.

"It seems like you got through yesterday okay, though." He slid a storage bin into the center of the room with his foot. I'd requested we take down the Christmas decorations early.

I stared at the Tardis tree ornament Tom bought in honor of Michael. "Maybe we lost the link because *I* can't figure out what I'm feeling." My arms dropped listlessly to my sides, a string of lights dangling in one hand. I was able to tell Tom when I was sad or angry, but beyond simple statements, I struggled to find the words.

What is it? Why am I so stuck?

Then it hit me. "We were never together with Michael for Christmas," I uttered.

Tom stopped packing his grandparents' miniature ornaments, a blank look on his face.

He doesn't understand. A bright, hot mass mushroomed in my stomach. "I don't have any memories and never will," I spat, my temper erupting like a geyser. I threw the tangled lights onto the coffee table and put my back to him; hot tears burst from my eyes. *Fuck. Fuck. Fuck.*

I wanted all the cheery holiday crap gone. Tom had insisted we put up decorations, saying it might ease my sorrow. It didn't.

I shook my head violently, trying to dispel the instant fury in my gut, and then stalked into the kitchen to grab a glass of water. My hand shook as I tried to gulp it down between ragged breaths, too angry to cry. Setting the half-empty glass down, I grabbed the edge of the counter, white-knuckled, and stepped one foot back, bending forward at the waist. I dropped my head between my outstretched arms, and I took several jagged gulps of air.

Tom had continued wrapping, and when I came in a few minutes later, he didn't say anything—he was well-practiced in waiting out my silences.

"David was on my mind a lot yesterday," I finally volunteered. Just thinking about him brought an immediate shift from anger to compassion. *Why can I feel sympathy for David but not myself?*

"What were you thinking?"

"Just wondering how he's holding up; how they're all holding up." My shoulders wilted as the anger vanished as quickly as it had risen. Absently, I reached down to pick up the lights again, twisting them in my hands.

"You could write to him; see how he's doing."

I shrugged and returned my attention to the lights.

The next day, while Tom was at work, I roamed the house, moving from one end to the other. Luna sat on the couch, bulging eyes tracking my passage as I paced in and out of the living room. I wanted to know what happened at their house on Christmas. Did they set a place for Michael or hang his stocking, like one article I'd read suggested? Did David buy a gift Michael would have liked and give it to someone else? Did they laugh at shared memories and cry about his absence?

So many of the recommended coping techniques didn't apply to me. We'd never had a stocking for Michael. He'd never sat at my table. I didn't even know what he liked to eat.

And, hardest of all, I kept coming back to the fact that I didn't have any memories.

Self-pity rose like bile in my throat.

Then, on top of that, I hadn't even cried on Christmas Day.

What's wrong with me?

My skin crawled for every perceived horror I'd committed. They fell like dominoes, cascading into a litany of sins and regrets: I wasn't even a real mom. I didn't try hard enough to see him. I gave him away. I didn't deserve to miss him...

Finally, unable to endure any longer, I gave in to my grief. Collapsing on the bedroom floor, I curled my arms around myself and sobbed. My body ached as if bruised and battered from the raging battle inside. I surrendered and embraced every negative thought, every missed opportunity.

When the trembling subsided, I caught a glimpse of myself in the floor-length mirror. The face looking back reminded me again of the ginger-haired, freckle-faced girl I'd once been–vulnerable, needing tenderness. What I wanted more than anything was a mother's embrace. A soft hand to smooth strands of hair from my forehead and tell me everything was going to be all right. But I couldn't go to my mother.

But, maybe I could mother myself.

Compassion for that little girl overcame me, and with it, a realization: I'd been so hard on myself. I expected far more than I ever would have asked of another. My suffering was self-inflicted punishment for crimes no one else saw. And even if all the terrible things were true, they did not disqualify me from forgiveness, especially in the face of remorse.

I rocked backward as if struck. I squared my shoulders, lifted my head, and then crawled closer to the mirror. With both palms on the glass, I noticed shades of hazel in bloodshot eyes. I stared hard at my reflection and spoke aloud. "I don't want to ride this roller-coaster any longer. Everything is not all right, but I don't want to feel like this anymore."

I wanted to be rid of the self-critical person lurking beneath the confident, assertive, and resilient woman I knew I was inside. I needed to learn to hold myself in compassion's arms.

With a new clarity of mind, I spent the days before the new year scouring the Internet, yet again, for resources and suggestions. Resolving to find ways to make my life less miserable, I committed to transforming. Recovery was in my hands; I just needed to find bite-size tools to implement change.

Meditation, I read, could help reduce anxiety. One blog promised I'd feel a difference if I committed to one minute a day for seven days. So, I decided to try. First, I researched proper form. Do I sit or lie down? What about my eyes, open or closed? And my hands? Where do I put them? There were multiple suggestions and styles, and in the end, I just had to make an arbitrary choice.

I grabbed the egg timer from the kitchen counter, set it to one minute, and sat cross-legged on the floor. I straightened my spine, placed my hands palm down on my knees, and inhaled. As I exhaled, trying to dispel all the air from my lungs, I closed my eyes. When the alarm sounded, I was thinking about what to make for dinner.

Resetting the clock, I closed my eyes to try again. This time when the bell rang, I was deep into plans for tomorrow morning's workout. *Argh!* Once more, I set the timer and decided to count my breaths. It worked. Six breaths. *Success!*

Each day for a week, I sat and breathed. Despite frequent distractions and getting angry with myself, I *was* calmer and more focused, just enough to spur me onward. The following week, I signed up for free guided meditations. Regardless of the difficulty and my limited success, I was hooked. Already, fantasies of sitting for twenty or even thirty minutes—because as a perfectionist, more is always better—filled my mind. Sometimes being an over-achiever can be an advantage.

Another article explored the role of self-compassion in quality of life. It recommended two specific activities.

First, to think about someone I felt strong compassion toward, then try to shift those feelings to myself. I chose David. Whenever I thought about the losses David had endured, my whole body softened. So, I began by envisioning David at the cemetery, then placed myself next to him, and kept both our images in my mind's eye. I visualized the empathy I extended to David as a glowing orb, expanding it to encompass me as well.

The second activity seemed dismissively easy. It wasn't.

I switched on the bathroom light and stepped in front of the mirror. Arms limp at my sides, I stared into my reflection. My red hair, parted on the side, framed my face in waves, softening the angles of my square jaw. Attempting to ignore the flaws—the wisps of grey, a zit, the un-plucked brows—I focused. The dark rings around my hazel eyes stood out in sharp contrast to my ruddy complexion. I leaned in, placed my hands on the basin, and prepared to speak, then flinched, pushing back from the glass.

"I love you," I choked before losing my nerve. The immediacy of my tears shocked and horrified me.

"I love you," I gasped, wanting desperately to sound sincere.

"I love you, I love you, I love you." Each repetition took on a new inflection. Slowly and softly, as if speaking to a slumbering infant, then with the urgency of parting lovers. Over and over, I repeated these three words, crying bitter tears that something so simple could be so hard.

To this day, I still tear up when I find the courage to do this exercise.

Journaling was touted as one of the best self-help tools, and I knew from experience it worked to increase self-esteem and boost clarity. And I always loved writing, so it wasn't hard for me to pick up a pen. This time though, I used the computer.

Right from the beginning, however, I confronted a conundrum. How can I explain my grief over the loss of a child I didn't even know? So, I began free writing. Anything goes, no holds barred; just let the words flow without concern for spelling, grammar, or punctuation. And when I went back to read what I'd written, I discovered a pattern. For every aspect of my sorrow at his death, I found a corresponding pain obscured within his adoption. And even more profound, grief for an abused little girl and an abandoned young woman. The trauma and suffering throughout my life tangled together in a knotted skein.

The fact that I'd never get the chance to watch *Dr. Who* with Michael became intimately tied with the fact that we never watched any movie or TV show together. Missing out on spending this past Christmas with him reminded me I'd never seen him over any holiday. And accepting that he'd never hike a trail with us reminded me we'd never done anything recreational together—never had and never would.

My grief wasn't just about his death but also his adoption. These losses were tied together in a way I hadn't been able or willing to recognize until then, and I couldn't deal with one loss without ad-dressing the other.

My knee-jerk reaction to withdraw or avoid emotional pain remained, so I had to find another way. A memory on Michael's Facebook page gave me the first opportunity. It triggered a bout of heated jealousy, and I caught myself clenching my fists and holding my breath. I loosened my hands, one finger at a time, and focused on the sensations in my body instead of the emotions in my head. Later, I wrote what I'd been thinking and feeling from the distance of time.

One evening, in early January, while we sat on the floor in the living room with dinner spread out on the coffee table, I turned to Tom. "I'm thinking about starting a blog."

He nodded with his mouth full.

"I've been writing a lot about Michael. And, you know how hard I find it to articulate what I'm feeling, right?" He tipped his head forward and raised his eyebrows in his duh expression. "Well, it seems to help me sort things out, and a blog would let me share it with others, but at a safe distance." I put air quotes around safe.

"Do it," he said, without hesitation, nodding as if it were the most logical thing in the world. My head snapped back. How does he come to conclusions so quickly about things I agonize over?

"Would you read what I'm working on?"

"Of course," he said, stabbing another forkful of salad. "Do you want me to add any feedback or editing or anything like that?"

"Only if you want to. Mostly, I just want to share it."

"You should send it to my mom, too. I'm sure she'd love to help."

I poured my energy into building an online page, embracing the job with passion, devotion, and desperation. The logistics of creating a blog piqued my interest and satisfied the need for a goal. The writing proved cathartic in that it helped me explore my feelings and triggers to find patterns and rewarding because it gave me an outlet to create something beautiful, even if tragically so.

If I could share my grief and the insights I'd discovered to survive, maybe I could help someone else navigate the pain of child loss. I'd felt so alone in my sorrow after Michael's adoption. And then, after his death, I'd discovered that no matter how someone might lose a child, the grief is universal. And I wanted them to know that they were not alone no matter their circumstances.

"Have you thought about what you're going to name your blog?" Tom asked several days later.

"Yep. Here," I handed him the laptop.

Along the top of a newly designed webpage ran the title and subtitle: *Lost Again: One woman's journey through the loss of her son. First placed in an open adoption, then through his sudden death 23 years later.*

I reached over his forearm to the computer, switching to a Word document. "This is going to be my first post."

> *I lost my son.*
> *He died this past July.*
> *He was only 23.*
> *It's not the first time. I placed him for adoption as a newborn.*
> *That loss was the hardest thing I've ever been through in my life.*
> *Until now.*

He turned his face to mine, a glassy glint in his eyes, "Perfect."

I uploaded that first post the next day. Then, after completing a lengthy introduction for my profile page, I published snippets of my myriad struggles, sharing both my successes and failures.

I organized my blog posts into three categories: "Lost Again," "On Being a Birth Mother," and "Ponderings." "Lost Again" posts centered on my grief surrounding Michael's death and covered things like navigating birthdays and anniversaries, depression, anxiety, and learning to adapt to a new normal. The category, "On Being a Birth Mother," focused on memories from his birth and the adoption process, my struggles to accept my choices, and learning to embrace motherhood. And "Ponderings" encompassed a hodgepodge, any topic that didn't fit in the first two, as well as poetry and photographs. This one is from August 2014:

> *I glimpsed you like a ray of light in the forest*
> *soft, golden, fleeting*
> *you cast shadows too*
> *yet they hold no meaning for me.*
> *As you play your music*
> *I hear the past,*
> *see the future,*
> *feel the moment…*

I feel the moment.
Dappled leaves flutter gently in the breeze
you walk with me... hold my hand
gravel crunches below my tired and swollen feet
road signs are trees and boulders; you'll find no words here.
The rain and sun have conspired to nourish my soul
I smell salt in the air, and change to come
the trees that bow to the prevailing winds still grow strong
I will too.

Over the next couple of years, I began to see and feel the changes that resulted from my self-improvement efforts. I discovered I was less anxious and self-critical and linked it back to my meditation practice. By focusing on the present moment rather than remaining locked in my past mistakes, I could be intentional about how best to move forward. The fear of my strong emotions lessened as I slowed down, examined which beliefs triggered the feelings, and chose which thoughts I would invest in and what actions I would take. Instead of staying stuck in the "I am a bad mother for giving my son away or for not trying harder," I could change the internal dialogue to "you did the best you could at the time with the resources and information you had available." This shift both reduced stress and created the opportunity to show myself compassion. The benefits I attributed to my efforts at self-improvement resulted in a desire to perpetuate those good feelings. I expanded my morning meditation to twenty minutes or more, but only after realizing a small cushion under my tailbone made sitting more bearable, and I added a daily yoga prac-tice and a morning gratitude habit—small but mighty steps. But no matter how much time I spent on the cushion or how consistent my practices, something would invariably trigger me and I'd revert to old patterns and behavior.

CHAPTER 27

Two Years Later—October 2015
Would Have Been 25 Years Old

Ceilings soared, and countless rooms split off in odd directions, like an Escher painting. Dozens of people milled about, the hum of conversation, like a weight, penetrated the corners and hallways. In each room, a distinct style of television—an old console tv, a theater-size flat screen, a square picture-tube model—played home movies. In one, four-year-old Michael sat in front of a Christmas tree; in another, pre-teen Michael on vacation with his dad, his hair dyed goth-black, posed in front of the Grand Canyon, smiling.

I roamed from room to room, slowly at first, then broke into a run, worried I'd miss something. In every image, garnered from some story I'd heard or photo I'd seen, a scene from Michael's life showed the fullness, comfort, and love of his lived experience. And although I couldn't see Michael, I felt his presence and heard a disembodied voice say, "I had a good life. A great life. I didn't need you."

I woke, surging upright, as muted moans escaped my lips. This was my first dream about Michael since he died. I clasped my hand to my chest, the words, *I didn't need you,* echoing in my ears. I struggled to stifle my cries and prayed no one heard me. Julie and I, and a few others, were kayaking down the Rose River in Northern British Columbia.

I stuffed a corner of my sleeping bag into my mouth and let the tears slide down my cheeks to darken the polyester shell. After the erratic gulps of air evened out, I unzipped my tent and slipped out.

My breath billowed and hovered briefly before dissipating into the crisp dawn air. Hints of snow dotted the ground and outlined the forest boundary just beyond camp, where a squirrel scolded me from a tree branch. Down at the river's edge, a thin layer of ice had formed in the shallows, reaching like fragile fingers into the faster flow. I sat cross-legged on the sandy bank, pictured myself floating upon the water, and surrendered to my sadness. My grief had subsided since Michael's passing, manifesting less like tsunamis and more like gentle swells and bubbles, tumbling over river rocks.

This dream presented an image of the reality that Michael's life, without me, had been good. David was an amazing father, and despite Jane's death, Michael had thrived. I needed to accept this but still struggled to. Sometimes, it seemed grief was all I had left of Michael, and I clung to it with desperation.

CHAPTER 28

Two Months Later—December 2015
Would Have Been 25 Years Old

Tom snapped his recliner into the upright position, catapulting him forward. He spun toward me, "Do you realize what you just said?" I wilted and turned away.

His voice softened, "It's the first time I've ever heard you say that. It's a big deal."

We were talking about regret, specifically Tom's, for keeping me from reaching out to Michael after our reunification. He wished he hadn't held me back from contacting him.

"You were right, though." I'd said and faced him.

He'd raised his eyebrows, disbelief written on his face.

"Really, Tom, I would have become obsessive and overbearing and scared him away. I agreed with you then and agree now."

He shook his head.

"I know you can't believe I don't blame you. But it was *my* choice to listen to you. Just like the adoption was *my* choice." I looked out the picture window and could no longer escape the truth. "But now, I wish...I wish I'd reached out to him more. Sent him more letters, pushed for more contact." Tears spilled down my cheeks, "I regret not trying harder."

That's when he'd bolted out of his chair. Now, he scooted close to me on the couch and placed an arm around my shoulders. I leaned into his embrace. Tears soaked into his flannel shirt. He remained quiet, waiting for me to find my voice.

"I hate that word," I said.

"What word?"

"Regret."

"Why?"

"Because to me, it means I made the wrong decision. And I can't," I gulped in air, "I can't be wrong—about placing him for adoption. It was the right thing at the time, for him, for me." The words caught in my throat. "Wasn't it the right thing?"

Lightheadedness and nausea swept through me. I swallowed, leaned forward, and placed my head in my hands, elbows on my knees. I shook my head from side to side and tried to dispel this new realization.

"Regret doesn't mean you were wrong." He gently rubbed my back. "And it doesn't make you a bad person."

Sobs voiced my disagreement.

Later that day, when Tom went back to work, I opened an on-line dictionary.

Merriam-Webster.com:

Regret: to feel sad or sorry about (something that you did or did not do); to have regrets about (something) -used formally and in writing to express sad feelings about something disappointing or unpleasant.

My head bent closer to the computer screen. I reread it. This definition was so much better than mine; it didn't limit regret to wrong versus right or enforce a dichotomy. Instead, it allowed for inclusiveness, and for the first time, my heart softened to a new reality.

Under this new-found definition, regret for relinquishing my parental rights while still maintaining it was the right choice could both be true. It was an epiphany. I repositioned my laptop on the desk and, purposefully, I typed:

I regret placing my son for adoption.

I wish I could have been his mom.

My chin dropped to my chest, my hair creating a curtain to block out the light, and I wept. I'd never admitted this before. In all the years between Michael's placement and our reunion, the few times I shared my adoption story, I always, always, always said I never regretted my decision. Never. It was a badge of honor, and I thought it prevented people from judging me.

The transition to viewing the adoption on a continuum that allowed two contrary things to be true at the same time opened the door for new perspectives concerning Michael. My anger about missing out on his childhood didn't negate my confidence that it was the right decision, just as my inability to be present and fulfill the role of mom did not nullify the fact that I remained a mother. He could have been angry with me and still want to know me. And I also began to rethink how I felt about Jane. Maybe she could have been a good mom despite having committed suicide. When I first learned about Jane's death, it felt like a punch in the gut. *How could she!* She'd abandoned Michael when he was ten years old, breaking her promise to me. I was horrified and outraged, but the shock of betrayal quickly gave way to the need to focus on the potential reunion with my son. David's letter had also contained details of Michael's life, effectively providing distractions from the horror of her suicide.

Then, as I built a relationship with Michael, I continued to block out what I viewed as Jane's betrayal. I didn't ask David about her death because I feared David, as gatekeeper, might block my ability to reach Michael. And the last thing I wanted to do was risk my connection to Michael. I've since learned that most first-parents fear asking for too much, knowing the adoptive parents could cut all ties to their children.

Only once, I mentioned Jane around David. It was during our third weekend visit to David and Lori's house after Michael's death. David, Lori, Tom, and I had gone out to dinner at one of Michael's favorite restaurants and returned to the house for wine and conversation. It was late, and we'd had several bottles of wine. After retiring to the guestroom, Tom scolded me, "What did you say about Jane?"

"What do you mean?"

"Well, I heard you say Jane's name in a condescending tone of voice, but I didn't hear anything else."

"I just said we'd have to talk about her sometime. That I have unresolved feelings about her." Tom glared at me.

"Oh, come on. It wasn't that bad, was it?""Yeah, you sounded angry, and then David paled."

"Well, *I am* angry."

"That's not fair. You can't just spring something like this on David, especially after a night of drinking." He stood looking at me, waiting for me to acknowledge his point.

"Yeah, yeah, you're right." My shoulders sagged.

"And, yes, I know you're angry, but you always seem to conveniently disregard how terrible her loss must have been for David and the boys."

I rocked back as if slapped in the face.

"Besides, if you want to talk to him about Jane, you should have a plan for what you want to say and what you want to know."

"Yes, you're right. Again. Goddess, I get tired of you being right!"

We enjoyed coffee with David and Lori in the morning, with no mention of Jane, then visited Michael's grave before heading home.

As Tom drove, I absently scraped at the accumulated frost on the inside of the truck window with my fingernail. Little icy flakes floated down onto my sweater sleeve, leaving a wet patch when it melted.

Does it even matter now that Jane committed suicide?

"Hey, what's going on over there? I'm getting a weird vibe."

"Thinking about David. And Jane." I turned to look at Tom; his strong silhouette stood out in contrast to the snowy landscape beyond his window. "Wondering if I'd have chosen them as parents had I known about Jane's family history of depression."

"And?"

"I don't know. First of all, I'm not sure they even knew about it back then. I guess that would be one question to ask David. But, really, does it even matter?"

"I can't answer that."

"Even if I had known that history, I wouldn't have thought it would lead to suicide." I paused. "Besides, is there any good reason for me to pry into her death?"

"I think you have to ask yourself *why* you want to know."

"Yeah," I swung my gaze back to the window and resumed scraping the frozen condensation, which had built up again.

Yes, it's possible that if I'd known Jane had mental health concerns, I might not have chosen them. But David had written the perfect letter, and that document weighed heavily in my decision. In hindsight, I think it would have been enough. Besides, if hopeful adoptive parents were required to pass a health assessment prior to approval, would I have been notified? Unlikely.

"Do you think she was depressed before you gave Michael to them?"

"No. Or, at least I don't want to think that."

"Could it be that David thought another child would help?"

I shuddered, suddenly nauseous. *Was David just trying to fix things?*

I thought I'd chosen the perfect family, the perfect couple. But even this dream family couldn't escape life's ups and downs. Holding onto negative feelings toward Jane hurt David *and* me, and I was tired of hurting myself. Not only that, but Jane's suicide was tragic and had transferred her suffering to her husband and her sons. I could think of nothing sadder in the world.

"It changes nothing now," I said. "Michael's gone, and so is Jane. And besides, there's no such thing as a perfect family."

CHAPTER 29

Nine Months Later—August 2016
Would Have Been 26 Years Old

Plump blueberries and high-bush cranberries bordered the rug-
ged path, and bulbous king-bolete mushrooms, well past their
prime, decomposed on the forest floor. I hitched the nearly thirty-pound
backpack slightly higher, and then settled the weight more evenly
onto my hips. Tom had set a brisk pace along the historic Chilkoot
Trail, and we were already five miles into the thirty-three-mile hike.

"So, what's up?" Tom asked. "You've been surly and a pain in
the ass for weeks now."

Despite the heavy pack and the fact that he couldn't see me, I shrugged.

"I know it's easy for you to get caught up in the daily routine
and ignore stuff, so here we are." He turned mid-stride and waited
for an answer.

I brushed past him. "I don't know." Dark green spruce and lighter
hemlock branches filtered murky light from an overcast sky, casting
shadows over tree roots to create a disorienting pattern on the trail.
Although I'd made great strides in self-awareness, I still reverted to
old patterns of avoidance more often than I liked to admit.

"Aw, come on. What's been bugging you?" He kept pace behind me.

"I'm fine. F-I-N-E. Fine."

"Is it work?" He prodded.

"I… don't…know," my words clipped.

"The band?"

"No. I told you, I don't know!"

"Michael? Have you been thinking about Michael?"

"No. Yeah. I mean, yeah, I think about him a lot, but, no, it's not that. I've been feeling fairly good about him, although I don't think that's quite the best way to describe it." I dramatically flicked each foot out as I walked, like a petulant child.

"Is it your mom?"

I reached up with one hand, grabbed hold of a cottonwood branch, and yanked on it. I stopped abruptly, faced the tree head-on, and with both hands violently wrenched on the limb, generating enough force to shake the whole tree.

Like a cornered animal, I half groaned, half screamed. The backpack straps dug into my shoulders from the tension of my biceps, while the bag's weight hindered my movement.

Tom stepped back, giving me a wide berth.

I slipped the pack from my shoulders, let it fall on its side, and swung my arms like a windmill, hitting the branches over and over. Minutes passed as I unleashed my aggression onto the innocent cottonwood. The leaves rustled against each other before fluttering soundlessly to the ground. Finally spent, I hung my head.

"So, your mom, then?"

"I still can't believe she came to Michael's funeral!" I crumpled to my knees mid-trail, head in hands. "She said he was dead to her."

"Oh, sweetie." Tom kept his distance. I don't know if he feared another violent outburst or just wanted me to continue talking. "What else are you mad about? This explosion feels bigger than that."

I stilled, my hands now rested on my knees, and I stared blankly into the forest. "She didn't protect me," I said, my voice a mere whisper, flat and despondent. "Gene, the sexual abuse. She didn't protect me from him."

The words bubbled up then, erupting like lava.

"And every time I've tried to talk to her about it, she cries. And then it becomes about *her*, how terrible it is for her, how *she's* a failure, and *her* sadness that it all happened. Then, I can't help myself; I immediately move to comfort her, instead of her comforting me!" I turned to face him, "That's how it always plays out. Always."

He took a tentative step toward me but remained silent.

"Sometimes, I think she knew it was happening." A storm raged in my gut. "But other times, I don't know. She kept seeing him after they split. Did I tell you that? Even after the divorce. Once, I woke to find them sleeping together on the sofa-bed in that piece-of-shit basement apartment we could barely afford, his drunken breath and grotesque body odor permeating the living room." I gagged. "That stench…it transported me back to my childhood bedroom…"

Tom approached. I felt his presence near me, quiet, waiting.

"She never, not once, said she was sorry."

He placed a hand on my shoulder. I raised my eyes, now clear, and gave him my hand, and he helped me to my feet.

Collecting me in his arms, he said, "I know she wasn't a good mom and isn't now. It doesn't make her a bad person. But you can't keep expecting her to act differently. She doesn't have the capacity."

My cheek rested against his neck, and I felt the words resonate in his chest as he spoke.

"I'm sorry," he continued, "but you have to accept that she will never be the mother you want her to be. Then, decide how you want to proceed."

He made it sound so simple. So easy.

"But how? I mean, I love her. I've always loved her. She's my mom. But I'm so angry. I don't want to be, but I am."

"You can be angry at her and love her at the same time."

"What?"

"Yes."

My shoulders slumped, and I stared at him. Hell, it never occurred to me that it was okay to be mad at Mom. I never thought I could feel both simultaneously. The forest seemed to brighten. I grabbed my pack and hefted it onto my back.

We hiked for a while in silence as I processed Tom's words.

"Should I call her?" I asked, plodding along behind him.

"Do you want to?" He said over his shoulder.

"Yes. And no. I miss her. We've hardly spoken the past three years."

"What is it you want to say?"

"I want…I don't know. I want us to at least talk."

"About?"

"Stuff. Life. Not about the abuse or Michael. But I want us to have a relationship." I knew there were still issues to confront concerning the abuse, but I minimized their importance, focusing instead on how I could talk to Mom. *One step at a time.*

"Why?"

"Because she's my mom, and I love her."

"Okay. But I don't want you to get hurt or set yourself up for failure."

"I'll only call her when I'm feeling strong and capable of dealing with her moodiness. I know I can't take her criticism and irritability, but we can talk if she's civil. Set some boundaries, I guess."

"Maybe when you call, assess her state of mind, and if she seems crabby, tell her you just called to say hi and that you love her and then hang up. If she seems okay, then you can talk. What do you think?"

"That could work." Sparks of optimism flared in my heart.

"Why don't you call her when we get home and see what happens, and then take it one call at a time." He abruptly stopped mid-trail, "Geez, I sound like a dork." He turned to look back at me, a smile playing on his lips, "And you know, you can always share *my* mommy?"

After we returned from the three-day hike, I called Mom. It had been almost two months since we'd last spoken.

"Cand? Oh, hi, honey! It's so good to hear your voice!" Tension drained from my body at the lightness of her tone.

"Hi Mom, how are you?"

Labored huffs punctuated her words, "My COPD (Chronic Obstructive Pulmonary Disease) is getting worse." She paused. "I've been going to classes at the senior center for people with breathing issues. They are teaching me better breathing techniques."

"Do the exercises work?"

"I guess, a little." She snorted. "I don't know how they think I'm supposed to *take deep breaths;* I have COPD, for heaven's sake! And there's this one woman, Sheryl—I think that's her name—she's so high and mighty, looking down on the rest of us like we're dog poop on her shoe. Oh, and my gosh, the old stogies in that class, some of them are so crotchety!"

Trying not to snort myself, I said, "I'm glad you're trying, Mom."

"What about you, honey? When do you plan to come home?"

She'd never accepted that I considered Alaska my home, not Minnesota. I don't think she ever realized I'd moved to Alaska, at least partly, to escape her. "October or November. For a visit. Not sure of the dates yet."

"Maybe you can help me put in some new lights. My eyesight's been getting worse lately, and they recommend better lighting."

I paused, but only briefly, "Sure, I can help."

I knew the visit would proceed precisely as every visit had played out since I'd moved to Alaska. I would arrive, and she would pull out her honey-do list, which I would attack with gusto. When all items were complete, she would insist I sit down with her at the table and engage with one-hundred-percent concentration on her. She wanted to be the center of my world for as long as she could convince me to stay. It would be exhausting, but I was already committed just by offering to help. I also knew that she would launch into a lengthy tirade about my absence as soon as I got up to leave.

"I have appointments to see an ophthalmologist and a gastroenterologist next month."

"You should keep me posted."

"Oh, I don't want to be a bother." Classic Mom.

"No, please, call. I want to know how you are doing. If I'm busy, I won't answer. But I'll call you back, I promise." Her silence was a testament to my track record.

For years I had sent Mom's calls to voicemail and wouldn't call back for days because I never knew who I would be talking to: the sweet mom who told me she loved and missed me or the angry mom who was still pissed I'd left her to live with Tom in Alaska. Sweet mom was present only about thirty percent of the time.

So "New Candace" began calling Mom once a week and followed these guidelines: if she were kind, we would converse pleasantly, but if she answered with a note of harshness, I'd keep it short. Slowly, like a feral cat, she began to trust me and started phoning me first. I continued to use the voicemail trick if I wasn't in a stable mental space but tried to call back within a day or two.

The following month, the ophthalmologist diagnosed my mom, at the age of sixty-eight, with macular degeneration.

"I'm going blind," she said, fear evident in her voice. "Within the year. It's inevitable. What am I going to do?"

"I'm so sorry, Mom. I don't know."

Each subsequent phone conversation included a new litany of health issues punctuated by panic attacks and random outbursts at my siblings.

"Why won't they call me? You call me, why can't they? They hate me. You don't hate me, do you?"

"Mom, I love you. But you have to realize they have children and spouses and jobs. They're just busy. They're not trying to be mean." I knew why they didn't call. It was for the same reason I hadn't for years: Mom was exhausting. She was spiteful and petty yet demanded our undivided devotion and attention.

"I suppose you're right," she sighed dramatically.

"Do you remember when you had five kids at home? How you never seemed to have time for anything?"

"Uh-huh."

"Well, they are experiencing that same thing themselves now. Try to give'em a break, okay?"

"All right, I will."

"So, what does your page-a-day calendar say today?" I'd become a master of deflection, redirecting Mom's focus when she became irritable. Her daily calendar, which had graced the kitchen table for as long as I could remember, was a perfect tool. Each year offered a new topic: bible verses, motivational sayings, vocabulary building. This year was affirmations, for which I was profoundly grateful.

It was at this point, though, with the diagnosis of blindness, that I made the conscious decision to protect my mother, if I could, from any additional suffering. I vowed to give her the love and support I'd always sought from her, and I would do my best, from the safety of Alaska, to ease her loneliness and fear and help her navigate the impending loss of independence.

A CHF (Congestive Heart Failure) diagnosis followed a complicated and grueling hernia surgery less than six months later. Her frail body struggled with a wound that wouldn't heal, so my siblings and I put our heads together on a conference call, trying to decide the best course of action.

"She's pissed at me," hissed my brother, Miles, the thickness of his voice sounded both sad and angry.

"Why?" Stacy asked.

"Because I authorized resuscitation during the surgery."

I gasped. Mom had a DNR, do not resuscitate, order. "Miles…"

"I know, I know, but this was different. This was surgery, right? I mean, her DNR has to do with finding her at home after a fall, or some other situation, not surgery." His voice pleaded for understanding. He had power of attorney for Mom, and it weighed heavily on his shoulders.

"Well, Miles, maybe you should take a step back and keep out of her way for a little while," Maggie said. "What should the rest of us do?"

"I'll take off work and come up to care for her for the first few days after she gets out of the hospital," Stacy, a Registered Nurse, offered. "I can manage a few days." Her tone indicated manage meant dealing with Mom, not taking time off work.

"That would be great," Maggie, the youngest said.

She lived the closest to Mom, just two miles away. "I'll take over after that. I'll go by a few times a week, buy her groceries, clean her apartment, cut her nails, stuff like that. The girls can come with me as a buffer."

"Sorry guys, but there's not much I can do from here. I'll try to call her every day, though, and try to lift her spirits," I volunteered.

"Shit, aren't you the brave one?" Bobby hadn't said much. He and Mom were on the outs about something, but none of us knew exactly what.

"Yeah, you can have that honor," Stacy mocked. "You're her favorite right now."

"Oh, yeah, what a privilege that is," I conceded, but deep down, I felt grateful. I had a way to contribute. And Mom would need me more now than ever.

During the summer, I called her on my walk to the gallery, saying hello and gauging her mood. If she sounded anxious or sad, I'd call her again over lunch or after work, sometimes both. When I was at home in the winter, I could more leisurely chat about movies, music, and memories. I tried to get her interested in books on tape, but she adamantly refused, preferring to listen to classical music and sometimes a little rock and roll. I even played guitar and sang for her a few times.

As Mom's health progressively deteriorated, she became increasingly fearful. Her inability to breathe triggered daily panic attacks. The COPD blocked her ability to inhale oxygen, and the CHF prevented her from expelling carbon monoxide. She was slowly suffocating, and the fact that she could no longer see magnified her dread. I received phone calls at all hours of the day and night, and all I could do was listen and try to help her calm down.

Yes, there were times during those dark days I was irritated by her constant need and didn't answer the phone, but I always called her back, usually within the hour. I consciously visualized myself in her shoes, connecting with how powerless and hopeless she felt, finally able to tap into the compassion I'd worked so hard to cultivate.

The years of meditation and the self-confidence skills I'd gained proved indispensable with Mom. I became the teacher as we practiced the same anxiety-reduction techniques I'd used myself. I adapted the five-senses grounding activity to four senses. I listened, phone tight to my ear, as she struggled to name four things she could touch, three things she could hear, two things she could smell, and one thing she could taste.

One of the most powerful habits I'd established was beginning each day by naming ten things to be grateful for, so I encouraged her to do the same. Even the smallest things counted. Research showed that even just the mental process of *searching* for something to be grateful for created greater happiness and comfort in day-to-day living. So, I'd wait, listening to her labored breaths. If she got stuck, I'd prompt, "What did you have for lunch today?" or "When was the last time Maggie came by?" I'd remind her of things like clean, abundant water right from her tap or her favorite coffee mug, things we often take for granted but which fill our daily lives with comfort and joy. Sometimes she'd harumph, but by the end of the conversation, she'd always be in a better state of mind.

I even attempted to lead her in meditations over the phone, with marginal success. Meditation is about the breath, and Mom could barely breathe.

I wanted to bring a heart filled with love and compassion to every interaction with my mother along with light and joy to each of her remaining days. I did my best to keep my voice uplifted and melodious, and when Mom's anger at the cruelty of life caused her to snap at me, I accepted it without complaint. But often, when I hung up the phone, the overwhelming sadness of her situation left me in tears.

One morning out of the blue, she asked, "Can I have a picture of Michael?"

My heart flipped. I swallowed, unsure of what to say.

"I have pictures of the other grandkids on my hutch, and, although I can't see them very well, I was hoping you'd send me one of Michael."

"Um, yeah, sure." I began to pace. "I have one of his graduation pictures. I could make a copy. Would that work?"

"That would be perfect. Can you make it five-by-seven? I have a frame already."

"Okay," I said on autopilot.

When I got off the phone, I went to my remembrance shelf and selected his senior picture. In it, he stood leaning against a tree, his black turtleneck sweater contrasting his fair complexion. Shaggy hair hung just above his eyes, his expression serious. The bitterness that I hadn't been present at his graduation had given way long ago to gratitude that I even had a copy of this photograph. I brought it into the kitchen, took it out of its frame, and smoothed it out on the counter.

The back gate creaked open, slammed closed, and Tom strolled in the door. He slipped his coat off and slung it over a dining room chair in one smooth motion as he walked toward me. "What? What's wrong?"

"Me. I'm wrong," I sighed. "Or I *was* wrong. I've just realized something that I should have long ago."

"Okay, come on then, what?" He seemed concerned, relieved, and irritated all at the same time.

"Mom's reaction to Michael's adoption; it was just her way of dealing with his loss."

"Ha! Really?"

I glared at him.

"I told you that years ago." His brows raised, then furrowed. "I'm sorry, but I did."

"I don't remember that," I whispered and picked up the photograph. "I can't believe I didn't see it."

"Hey, if you can see it now, that's what's important, don't you think?"

"I just never considered how she felt." My stomach roiled. I placed my palm over my forehead, squeezing my temples with my thumb and middle finger. "God, I'm so selfish. She'd just lost her grandchild, and all I could think about was me."

"Yeah, so you were selfish, but you were also young and naïve. We've all been there. Plus, you were in a tough situation. Give yourself a break." He turned and opened the refrigerator, grabbed an orange, and began peeling it; a bright, citrus smell filled the room. "Are you gonna talk to her about it?"

"I don't know. What would I say?"

"You could say you're sorry," he leaned his hip against the edge of the counter, then plopped an orange wedge into his mouth.

"Yeah…okay." I let the conversation fade as Tom rummaged in the fridge again.

When Mom received the copy of Michael's photograph, she thanked me but never said another word about him, and neither did I. I was ashamed of my behavior after Michael's placement. However, despite the recent years of learning to acknowledge and accept my feelings, I still avoided anything remotely difficult or painful with Mom. I told myself I didn't need to add stress to her remaining days and extended myself the grace required to let the issue rest. And my heart had softened. I'd come to see that Mom had faced many of the same societal pressures I had, but the difference was, I'd had more choices.

In the last year of her life, I tried to focus on memories of love, kindness, and shared joy, like the time when I was a girl she bought me a guitar. Or the afternoons together spent riding bareback through fields of clover. To this day, I have no idea how she found a way to pay for the instrument or my horse, but both experiences shaped my life-long love of music and the outdoors, and for that, I am grateful.

I never told Mom I forgave her, but I'd never told her I blamed her either. When she died on April 18, 2018, I was relieved her suffering was over, and thankful I'd found a way to bridge the divide between us.

In the end, I believe it was Michael who brought us together. Michael, whose first embrace in this life was in the arms of my mother, not mine. Michael, who in death helped me find a way to forgive her because once I forgave myself for my inability to be a good mother, I could extend the same absolution to Mom. And Jane.

If I deserved it, so did they.

CHAPTER 30

June 2018
Would Have Been 28 Years Old

❝I have a grand adventure planned for you today. As your personal tour guide and chauffeur"—I reached up with both hands and mimed fixing a bow tie—"I will take you on a journey up the South Klondike Highway, following the path of thousands of gold-seekers more than one hundred years ago during the Gold Rush."

My breath came out in little white puffs in the perpetually cold morning air on the Skagway cruise ship dock. A sky-blue Patagonia raincoat declared my new occupation: tour guide. I'd changed jobs the previous summer after the gallery unexpectedly closed, slipping with ease into the performance-driven role of driver-guide. I loved my new job. No schedules to make, no inventory to track, and no employees to babysit. But, perhaps best of all, I adored being in the outdoors all day.

It was three days before the summer solstice. Gulls screeched and dove overhead, and the marine layer had dissipated. The crisp alabaster outlines of the White Pass, Harding Glacier, and the Dewey Peaks pierced the cobalt-blue sky, creating the impression they were photo-shopped into the landscape.

Almost every day, I took a small private group out on a full-day tour into Canada. We would lunch in the Yukon Territories and visit Iditarod Musher Michelle Phillips's dog camp in British Columbia. Photo opportunities and hikes abounded, and although the route didn't change—there is only one road in and out of Skagway—I'd come to appreciate, and point out, the tiniest of shifts in the environment.

But today, I had a special group: David, Lori, John, and over a dozen other members of Michael's family. David and I had been planning for months, and neither one of us could stop smiling now that the day had finally arrived.

After a bright day filled with vast vistas and wildlife, including the rare sightings of both a black and a brown bear, I escorted the group to Kathy's house. Kathy had volunteered to host a soiree. Despite a long, active day, I squirmed excitedly as we drove through the hillside neighborhood. Wild clover and white-topped yarrow dotted the grassy edges of the driveway, with cars parked cockeyed along the uneven gravel. We circled along the side of the house to the wraparound deck that overlooked the city and gave a clear view of the cruise ships parked in the bay and the Upper Lynn Canal beyond. The Dewey Peaks rose 5,400 feet across the valley, their snow-capped tops blending into the late-day azure sky.

Spread out on the deck, card tables and chairs sat in small clusters, and smoke from a BBQ grill carried scents of grilled chicken and bratwurst. People milled about a long buffet table packed with a smorgasbord of foods, loading plates and slipping slices of cheese or cut fruit into their mouths as they chatted happily with each other.

"Hey everybody," I said, using my loudest speaking voice, "this is Michael's family." A cheer went up among the crowd, with hi's and hello's mixed in. Then, I turned to David, Lori, and the rest of the group, "This is…everybody." I smiled. "You guys know what to do: mingle on."

After we ate, David and I stood side-by-side on the balcony overlooking Skagway. "I wish Michael could have come here," I leaned on my elbow, chin cupped in my hand. All day long, I'd imagined Michael with us. I'd pictured him wrestling and joking with John or teasing David about being the old guy in the group. I fantasized about my place in the family and was pleased and honored when David and Lori insisted I join in family group photos.

David sighed. "Yeah, me too. But, you know, I think he's here in spirit."

I smiled. I had to agree. The day had been perfect: weather, scenery, wildlife, but mostly, the sensation of Michael's presence next to me in the passenger seat, embodied by his family.

"This is an amazing view," David said.

I nodded. "Kathy has one of the best views on the hillside."

"And all this food! What a feast. How did you manage it?"

"I've got some great friends," I said and raised my glass to Kathy and Carol, who stood at the other end of the deck.

"The other wonderful thing about this deck is there's room for the band." I swept my hand toward the makeshift stage set up in front of the greenhouse. "I'm gonna head over and get this party started. I hope you enjoy the music."

I watched from the stage as Michael's family mingled with my friends. The younger kids danced and grabbed tambourines and maracas, adding more flair to "Wagon Wheel" and "500 Miles," while the adults sang along to "Mustang Sally" and "Signed, Sealed, Delivered."

Two hours later, as they walked toward their ship after we'd said our goodbyes, I smiled through tears. I'd always hoped to share my life in Alaska, my friends, and my music with Michael, and sharing it with his family brought my wish full circle.

CHAPTER 31

January 2019
Would Have Been 29 Years Old

The following January, while Tom worked, I flew from Alaska to Minnesota alone. We'd sold the cabin and bought a house near Tom's folks in Henderson, Nevada, and I needed to move our belongings. I finished loading the rental truck early, so I messaged David to see if he and Lori were up for a last-minute visit.

Frigid temperatures and brisk winds couldn't dampen the anticipation of seeing them or excitement to spend Michael's birthday near him for the first time – he would have been celebrating his twenty-ninth in two days. As I sang along to the radio, I realized that, for the first time, I wasn't lapsing into fear of rejection or apprehension on the drive to Marshall. When I maneuvered the oversized rental truck into the cul-de-sac and saw David on the front step, as he'd been every time I'd visited, I practically sprinted to the door for one of his hugs.

We lingered over dinner and caught up on family gossip and holiday activities, and it seemed I was just another family member home for a visit. Lying in bed that night, warm and cozy under one of Lori's quilts, I tapped into my gratitude. *I think it may be fate I'm here for his birthday.*

In the morning, David and I stood arm in arm in front of Michael's gravestone. The shiny black granite seemed infused with electricity, reflecting and refracting the light like a kaleidoscope, a perfect complement to the tiny sparkles atop the frosty snow. The wind whipped and snapped David's long overcoat like a pennant.

When David moved to Jane's headstone, I whispered to Michael, "I am so grateful you wanted to meet me and that we had that one beautiful day together." Tears, no longer fueled by regret, trickled down my cheeks. "And I love your dad. David is everything I hoped he would be, and I'm glad I'm getting the chance to know him and your whole family."

After we returned to the house, a seemingly endless progression of people stopped by to say hello, including John, who introduced me to his girlfriend. The revolving door of family and friends was a pleasant reminder of the loving and affectionate life Michael had lived, and I never tired of hearing stories about his escapades.

"Hey, why don't you come to visit me?" I asked as I prepared to leave the next day, "When you drive through Nevada on your road trip. Please? I have a bedroom waiting, and I'd love a chance to return your gracious hospitality."

And the following Wednesday evening at Applebee's, I grinned with delight when David and Lori showed up. I hugged them both and introduced them to Tom's sister, Kim, and his parents, Dee and Tom Sr.

When I'd told Dee earlier in the week that Michael's parents were coming for a visit, she'd clapped her hands joyfully. And as Dee embraced Lori in a hug, like long-time friends, and Tom Sr. shook hands with David, I nodded my head and wondered how I could be so lucky.

Laughter and banter filled the air as we dined, after which we retired to the house for a nightcap. When Lori and David continued their journey the next morning, we hugged and promised to see each other soon, knowing it wasn't an empty promise, but one built on the memory of our son and the fact that we are family.

After they left, I lounged on our back porch with my feet on the ottoman, coffee cup in hand. An early morning haze obscured the foothills and mountains in the distance, creating a watercolor in tawny sepia tones that stretched as far as I could see. The palm trees high overhead swayed gently in the breeze, a soft swish to accompany the calls of a covey of quail under the nearby lantana bush.

While I relaxed, I reflected on Michael's influence in my life. He, more than anything else in my world, despite his physical absence, had shaped who I am. He was the reason I scrutinized my reality as a young woman, assessed my capabilities and faults, and then made the conscious decision to change my trajectory. His existence propelled me to seek an education and find a respectable job. He even exerted influence from the womb. He is the reason I ended up in Tom's loving arms. In death, he continues to guide me. Would I have developed self-compassion without him? Forgiven my mother? Forgiven Jane? Forgiven myself?

I sighed and picked up my guitar. I plucked and hummed softly and then began one of my favorite Pink Floyd songs. For some reason or other, I hadn't learned to play it until recently.

Oh, how I wish, how I wish you were here.
We're just two lost souls swimming in a fishbowl, year after year,
Running over the same old ground.
What have we found?
The same old fears.
Wish you were here.

EPILOGUE

Dressing up as a clown on the Fourth of July provides me uninhibited joy. When I put the costume on, I transform into a new person, no longer afraid, self-conscious, or judgmental. Worry-free, I wholeheartedly embrace being silly and goofy.

But in the years following Michael's death, I dreaded the thought of donning my costume. I couldn't see past the image of a woman, collapsed in the middle of the street, dressed in that clown costume. The first two years after his death, I reluctantly put it on and paraded down Broadway, but behind those enormous sunglasses, tears flowed. So, on the third anniversary of Michael's death, I retired my fuzzy bunny slippers and girly clown outfit and ordered a new costume, one with striped pants, polka dot socks, and wide suspenders. I still wanted to clown around; I just didn't want to cry anymore while doing it.

I know Michael, a budding street performer, would have delighted in the joy and smiles brought to so many people, not the least of all to me, which is why I didn't give away my original costume. It's tucked in the back of the spare-room closet, covered in a dry cleaner's sleeve, with the hope that I would one day have the strength and courage to wear it again. I like to dream that had Michael lived, he would have joined me in skipping, hopping, and cartwheeling down the street.

And that image makes me smile.

Afterword

I didn't know David had sent us an email the morning of July 4, 2013, regarding Michael's death, until the summer of 2019. It was after I decided to write this book. I'd collected all the correspondence among David, Michael, and Tom and I into a single Word document. When I read this letter for the first time, my heart ached anew, for both David and I, but rather than inconsolable sorrow, all I felt was gratitude.

> *Thursday, Jul 4, 2013, at 6:46 AM*
> *Candace and Tom,*
> *I am reaching out to you with some very sad news. Michael has passed away. We were notified on Tuesday that he passed away and we are not sure what happened. I wanted to let you know Candace what a wonderful gift you gave me and my family when you allowed Jane and I to adopt Mike. I was so very proud of him as a person. Very loving, caring, and respectful. His inquisitive mind made him very special and at times entertaining. Sorry to leave you with this news.*
> *Michael was very happy getting to know you in his understanding of who he was. He was very much at peace with who he was as a person. Very self-confident.*
> *I am leaving my phone numbers if you would like to talk.*
> *My love and prayers go out to you guys during this very difficult time.*
> *Dave*

AUTHOR'S NOTE

The seeds of this memoir began during the early days of our reunion as I struggled to develop a relationship with my adult son. I sought out the stories of others who'd come before—first mothers and adoptees—in hopes they would provide guidance. There were so few. Society seemed focused on the "rainbows and unicorns" of adoption, with pictures of happy, fulfilled couples cradling new-borns and messages that first mothers are brave and selfless. But an alternate narrative, quieter and less intrusive, included adult adoptees and first parents addressing the trauma of abandonment and life-long mental health issues, giving me my first glimpse out of "the adoption fog." Then, in the aftermath of my son's death, I searched again for examples of how to endure the loss and found support through groups like The Compassionate Friends. Their focus, however, tended to be on traditional family structures and did not address ambiguous and disenfranchised grief like mine. So, I continued my search and finally found a commonality among those struggling with infertility and miscarriage. Their grief, like mine, was not openly discussed nor understood, and it was at this point I pledged to use my voice and experience to help start a conversation. It doesn't matter how you get here; the grief of child loss is universal.

I've done my best to depict events and people as honestly and realistically as possible. I relied on memory, years of correspondence, and journal entries to create an accurate account, but inevitably others will recall these same events differently. As with most memoirs, I've compressed time and approximated dialogue. Letters are transcribed from original correspondences, with minor editing for clarity.

ACKNOWLEDGEMENTS

To David for being an amazing father and encouraging me to share my story, *our* story. To Lori, John, Haley, Mikayla, and Michael's entire adoptive family – thank you for welcoming me into the fold and for your unconditional love. Special thanks to Hannah, who holds and shares so many memories, and Josh, whose kind words soothe my spirit.

To my friends and loved ones, I am forever in your debt. Thanks to Dee, Tom Sr., and Kim for your kindness, support, enthusiasm, and sharing Tom with me. To Julie, for listening patiently, asking tough questions, and sharing your unedited opinion: You have always been a model of strength, integrity, and attention to detail. To Steph, whose compassion, laughter, and vulnerability helped me find myself while setting the stage for a beautiful relationship. Thank you to Kathy, LC, and Charity for your friendship, kindness, and music: There's no one in the world with whom I'd rather play and sing. Carol's encouragement and professional perspective came together most beautifully, lifting me while keeping me focused. To Bea, Bob, and Kathy—gentle yet hardy spirits intertwined in love, sorrow, and mimosas—thank you for always greeting me with a smile. (The first words of this memoir were written in Bea's cabin on Lake Bennet.) Thank you, Julia, for braving the difficult content to share your experience as an adoptee. Lori, thank you for sharing your perspective as an adoptive mom, writer, and advocate for openness in adoption. Thanks to Lynne for editing assistance and Jeff (The North Words Writers Symposium) for answering questions on the fly, and your dedication to the arts. And to Bonnie, my cheerleader, ever willing to sit in meditation or have a glass of wine, usually both.

To the members of my memoir writing group, thank you for teaching me to write with feeling and precision while helping maintain my distinctive voice and style: Catherine Shields, Tammy Dietz, Cindy Langdon, Linda Jacqueline, Rachael Rauch, Bonnie Rost, Soorya Townley, Michelle Stewart Gardner, Kathy Whipple, Sheryll-Ann Odell, Stephanie Alison Carter, Susan A. Eames, Johnny Golightly, Rebecca Osequera, Claire Pankhurst, Emmy Wells, Diana Anyakwo, Bree Mosman, Alice Woodrome, Gregory D. Stevens, Rhonda Cronkhite, Mary Daurio, Krys Oxmind. Special thanks to On Your Feet Foundation and Concerned United Birthparents for grant funding. Thanks to the myriad people who influenced this work: Betsy Grava, Allison Lane, Anne Putnam, Allison Williams, Ashleigh Renard, Jana Maron, Pam Sheppard (Sheppard Editorial Services), and Sarah Nicolas. Bianca Marais, Carly Watters, and CeCe Lyra, of the podcast "The Shit No One Tells You About Writing," and Kristin Owens, Jami Carpenter, Latoya Smith. And to my writing networks: Skagway Arts Council, Henderson Writers Group, 49 Writers, and The Authors Guild.

And finally, Tom. Thank you for your gentle kindness, for always holding Michael sacred, for taking me on adventures I never dreamed possible, and for always believing I can achieve anything I set out to do. And especially for the intimate vacation in the Caribbean, when we were lounging at the beach, drinking Dos XX's, when you asked me what I would do if you were to pass. We'd just taken out life insurance policies – admitting we're getting older - and without hesitation, I said, "I'd find a little cabin somewhere overlooking a body of water and write a book." You'd gazed out at the water, then turned to me and asked, "Why wait?" So, thank you, Tom. I shudder to think what my life would have been like without you.

Please help other readers discover *Goodbye Again* by leaving a review on Goodreads and your favorite online book retailer.

Book Club
Discussion Questions

Candace is available through Zoom or Skype to meet with book groups to discuss *Goodbye Again.* If you're interested in having her as a guest at your book club, go to www.candacecahill.com/bookclubs

1. Candace's internal dialogue haunts her throughout the book. How do you think trauma affects one's inner critic? Do you have an inner voice, and if so, how does it impact your life?

2. What if Candace had been provided help and guidance to keep her son? Do you think she would have still succeeded in college, career, and love?

3. Candace named her son Foster Cameron. Do you think that made it harder for her to give him up?

4. What did you think about Candace's choice to stop requesting updates from the adoptive family? Why do you think it would be important to keep a dialogue open between a first and an adoptive family?

5. Was Candace right to listen to the advice to let Michael lead the way, or should she have pushed for more contact? Is there anything Candace could have done to better cope while waiting for Michael to take the next steps?

6. Do you think it would have benefited Candace to know when Jane passed away? Did you think Candace's feelings of betrayal were unjust?

7. For years Candace coped by stating that she didn't regret giving Michael up for adoption – that it was the best choice for him. How do you think Michael would have responded to hearing that?

8. Candace's mother's statement that Michael was "dead to her" played a significant role in their relationship - or lack thereof. If Candace had realized earlier that it was merely her mother's way to cope with the loss, do you think they would have reconciled earlier?

9. How important was it that Tom helped Candace view Michael's birthday and Mother's Day as celebrations? Do you think she ever would have done so without his help?

10. Do you think Candace held ill will toward her mother for being the first person to hold her son? Do you think it impacted their relationship?

11. Candace developed a close relationship with David. What do you think about their relationship? If Jane had lived, do you think Candace would have developed a close relationship with her as well, or would Candace have always treated Jane as "the other mother"?

12. Should Candace have sought professional help? Should Tom have encouraged her to get counseling? What could have helped Candace through the trauma of child relinquishment?

13. Had Candace not made it to Michael's funeral in time, how would that have impacted the relationship between her and David? Do you think she could have ever healed without the help and support of Michael's adoptive family?

14. Why do you think Candace called her mom from the airport to tell her of Michael's death?

15. Do you think Candace should have tried to prevent her mother from coming to the funeral to lessen her distress?

16. Why do you think it took Candace so long to differentiate between being a good mother and being a good person and coming to forgive her mother and herself?

17. Although Candace avoids referencing abandonment issues from her biological father, how do you think that affected her inner voices after placing Michael for adoption?

18. What are some examples of the dichotomies, two things being true at one time, in this memoir? Do you have examples from your own life?

ABOUT THE AUTHOR

Candace Cahill is a first mother and an LDA—late step-discovery adoptee. She grew up in rural Central Minnesota with no running water or electricity, and by the time she graduated from high school, she'd learned books were an oasis and her guitar a good friend. After earning a Social Work degree, she embarked on a year-long bicycle trip across North America before settling in Alaska. She is a self-taught silversmith and can play five instruments. Candace resides with her husband, Tom, in Denali, Alaska, and works as a Park Ranger during the summer months. Find out more at candacecahill.com.

CPSIA information can be obtained
at www.ICGtesting.com
Printed in the USA
LVHW030338261022
731543LV00004B/160